GOLF

By

Les Bolstad

Ellen Griffin

Barbara Rotvig

Bob MacDonald

ATHLETIC INSTITUTE SERIES

STERLING PUBLISHING CO., Inc. New York

ATHLETIC INSTITUTE SERIES

ARCHERY
BADMINTON
BOWLING
COMPETITIVE SWIMMING
DIVING
FENCING
GIRLS' GYMNASTICS
GOLF
LIFESAVING
SKATING ON ICE
SKIN & SCUBA DIVING
SOCCER
SWIMMING
TABLE TENNIS
TENNIS
TRACK AND FIELD
TRAMPOLINING
TUMBLING
VOLLEYBALL
WRESTLING

Foreword

The photographic material in this book has been reproduced in total from the National Golf Foundation's sound, color slidefilm, "Beginning Golf." This book and the slidefilm are parts of a program designed to bring the many benefits of athletics, physical education, and recreation to everyone.

The National Golf Foundation is a non-profit organization founded in 1936 to aid municipalities, educational institutions and private enterprise in stimulating greater interest in golf and increasing opportunities for participation in the game.

It is their hope, and the hope of The Athletic Institute, that through this book, the reader will become a better golf player, skilled in the fundamentals of this fine game. Knowledge, and the practice necessary to mold knowledge into playing ability, are the keys to real enjoyment of playing golf.

Published by Sterling Publishing Co., Inc.
419 Fourth Avenue, New York 16, New York

Manufactured in the United States of America
Library of Congress Catalog Card No.: 64-24680

CONTENTS

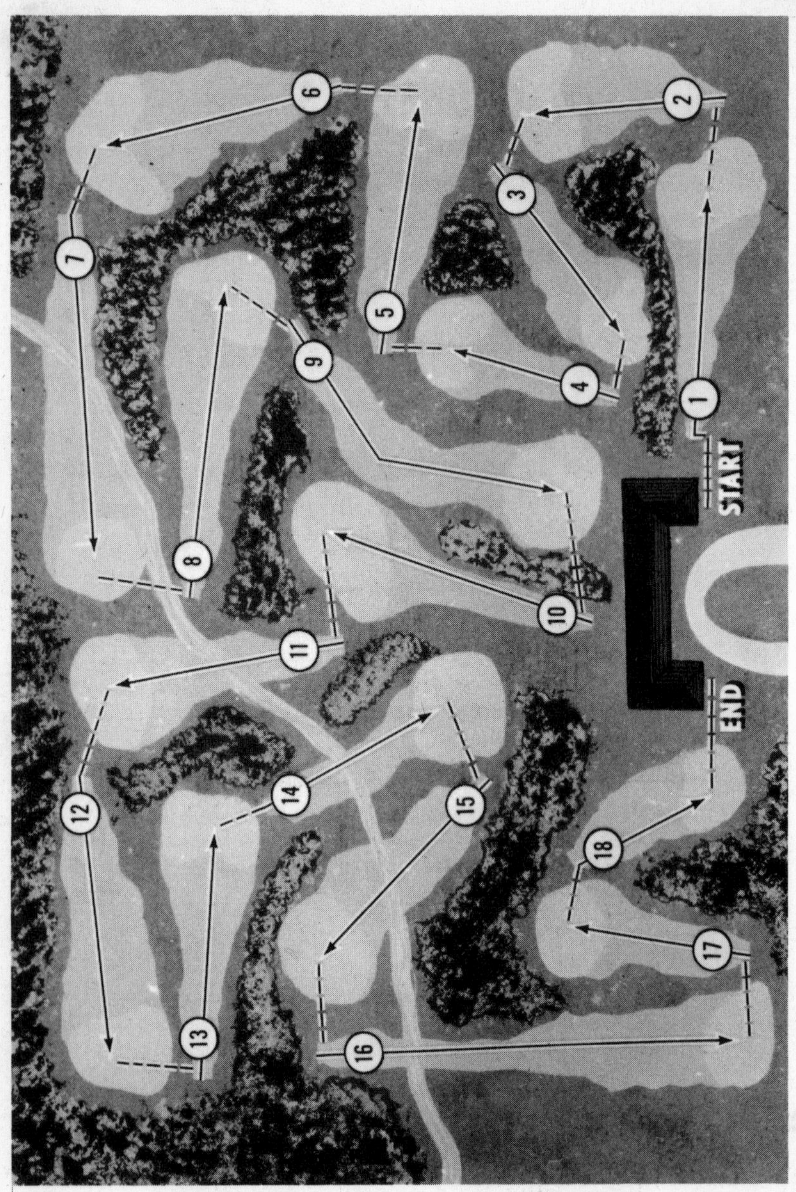

BIRDSEYE VIEW OF TYPICAL 18 HOLE GOLF COURSE

GLOSSARY

Addressing the Ball—A player has "addressed the ball" when he has taken his stance by placing his feet on the ground in position for and preparatory to making a stroke and has also grounded his club, except that in a hazard a player has "addressed the ball" when he has taken his stance preparatory to making a stroke.

Advice—"Advice" is any counsel or suggestion which could influence a player in determining his play, the choice of a club, or the method of making a stroke.

Information on the Rules or Local Rules is not "advice."

Approach—A stroke to putting green.

Away—Ball farthest from hole—to be played first.

Ball Deemed to Move—A ball is deemed to have "moved" if it leave its position and come to rest in any other place.

Ball Holed—A ball is "holed" when it lies within the circumference of the hole and all of it is below the level of the lip of the hole.

Ball in Play—A ball is "in play" as soon as the player has made a stroke on the teeing ground. It remains in play as his ball until holed out, except when it is out of bounds, lost, or lifted or another ball is substituted in accordance with the Rules or Local Rules.

Ball Lost—A ball is "lost" if:—

a. It is not found within five minutes after the player's side or his or their caddies have begun to search for it;

b. After a search of five minutes the player is unable to identify a ball as his ball.

Time spent in playing a wrong ball is not counted in the five-minute period allowed for search. Play of a wrong ball does not constitute abandonment of the ball in play.

Birdie—One stroke under the par of a hole.

Bogey—An arbitrary standard, supposedly based upon average good play; usually one stroke per hole higher than par.

Caddie, Forecaddie and Equipment—A "caddie" is one who carries or handles a player's clubs during play and otherwise assists him in accordance with the Rules.

A "forecaddie" is one employed by the Committee to indicate to players the position of balls on the course, and is an outside agency (Definition 22).

"Equipment" is anything used, worn or carried by or for the player except his ball in play.

Casual Water—"Casual water" is any temporary accumulation of water which is visible before or after the player takes his stance and which is not a hazard of itself or is not in a water hazard. Snow and ice are "casual water" unless otherwise determined by Local Rule.

Committee—The "Committee" is the committee in charge of the competition.

Competitor—A "competitor" is a player in a stroke competition. A "fellow-competitor" is any player with whom the competitor plays. Neither is partner of the other.

In stroke play foursome and four-ball competitions where the context so admits, the word "competitor" or "fellow-competitor" shall be held to include his partner.

Course—The "course" is the whole area within which play is permitted. It is the duty of the authorities in charge of the course to define its boundaries accurately.

Divot—Piece of sod cut by player's club (always to be replaced and pressed down).

Down—The number of holes or strokes a player is behind opponent. See "Up."

Eagle—Two strokes under par for a hole.

Fairway—Specially prepared, closely cropped area intended for play between tee and green.

Flagstick—The "flagstick" is a movable straight indicator provided by the Committee, with or without bunting or other material attached, centered in the hole to show its position. It shall be circular in cross-section.

Fore—A warning cry to any person in the way of play.

Green—The putting green.

Ground under Repair—"Ground under repair" is any portion of the course so marked by order of the committee concerned or so declared by its authorized representative. It includes material piled for removal and a hole made by a greenkeeper, even if not so marked. Stakes and lines defining "ground under repair" are not in such ground.

Handicap—Strokes given to equalize playing ability, usually based on player's best scores.

Halved—A hole is said to be "halved" when each side has played it in the same number of strokes.

Hazards—A "hazard" is any bunker or water hazard. Bare patches, scrapes, roads, tracks and paths are not "hazards."

a. A "bunker" is an area of bare ground, often a depression, which is usually covered with sand. Grass-covered ground bordering or within a "bunker" is *not* part of the "hazard."

b. A "water hazard" is any sea, lake, pond, river, ditch, surface drainage ditch or other open water course (regardless of whether or not it contains water), and anything of a similar nature.

All ground or water within the margin of a water hazard, whether or not it is covered with any growing substance, is part of the water hazard.

c. A "lateral water hazard" is a water hazard or that part of a water hazard running approximately parallel to the line of play and so situated that it is not possible or is deemed by the Committee to be impracticable to drop a ball behind the water hazard and keep the spot at which the ball last crossed the hazard margin between the player and the hole.

d. It is the duty of the Committee in charge of a course to define accurately the extent of the hazards and water hazards when there is any doubt. That part of a hazard to be played as a lateral water hazard should be distinctively marked. Stakes and lines defining the margins of hazards are not in the hazards.

Hole—The "hole" shall be 4¼ inches in diameter and at least 4 inches deep. If a lining is used, it shall be sunk at least 1 inch below the putting green surface unless the nature of the soil makes it impractical to do so; its outer diameter shall not exceed 4¼ inches.

Honor—The side which is entitled to play first from the teeing ground is said to have the "honor."

The right to drive or play first is determined by lowest score on preceding hole, by tossing coin on first hole.

Hook—The opposite of a slice. With a right-handed player it comes from a stroke which causes ball to rotate counter-clockwise and to curve to left of line from player to objective; with left-handed player spin imparted causes ball to go to right of line from player to objective.

Lie—The situation of a ball, good or bad. The "lie" of a club refers to the angle which the shaft makes with the ground when the club is sitting in its natural position.

Loose Impediments—The term "loose impediments" denotes natural objects not fixed or growing and not adhering to the ball, and includes stones not solidly embedded, leaves, twigs, branches and the like, dung, worms and insects and casts or heaps made by them.

Marker—A "marker" is a scorer in stroke play who is appointed by the Committee to record a competitor's score. He may be a fellow-competitor. He is not a referee.

A marker should not lift the ball or mark its position and, unless he is a fellow-competitor, should not attend the flagstick or stand at the hole or mark its position.

Match Play—Play in which each hole is a separate contest, winner being player or side winning most holes.

Observer—An "observer" is appointed by the Committee to assist a referee to decide questions of fact and to report to him any breach of a Rule or Local Rule. An observer should not attend the flagstick, stand at or mark the position of the hole, or lift the ball or mark its position.

Obstructions—An "obstruction" is anything artificial, whether erected, placed or left on the course except:

a. Objects defining out of bounds, such as walls, fences, stakes, and railings;

b. Artificially constructed roads and paths anywhere;

c. Any construction which is an integral part of the course, such as retaining walls of hazards and masonry on banks or beds of open water courses. (Bridges and bridge supports which are not part of water hazards are obstructions.)

Out of Bounds—"Out of bounds" is ground on which play is prohibited.

When out of bounds is fixed by stakes or a fence, the out of bounds line is determined by the nearest inside points of the stakes or fence posts at ground level; the line extends upwards. When out of bounds is fixed by a line on the ground, the line itself is out of bounds.

A ball is out of bounds when all of it lies out of bounds.

Outside Agency—An "outside agency" is any agency not part of the match or, in stroke play, not part of a competitor's side, and includes a referee, a marker, an observer, or a forecaddie employed by the Committee.

Par—The number of strokes a good player should need to play a hole without mistake under ordinary conditions; always allowing two putts on the green.

Partner—A "partner" is a player associated with another player on the same side.

In a threesome, foursome or a four-ball where the context so admits, the word "player" shall be held to include his partner.

Penalty Stroke—A "penalty stroke" is one added to the score of a side under certain Rules. It does not affect the order of play.

Press—To attempt to hit beyond one's normal power.

Putting Green—The "putting green" is all ground of the hole being played which is specially prepared for putting or otherwise defined as such by the Committee.

Referee—A "referee" is a person who has been appointed by the Committee to accompany players to decide questions of fact and of golf law. He shall act on any breach of Rule or Local Rule which he may observe or which may be reported to him by an observer.

In stroke play the Committee may limit a referee's duties.

A referee should not attend the flagstick, stand at or mark the position of the hole, or lift the ball or mark its position.

Rub of the Green—A "rub of the green" occurs when a ball in motion is stopped or deflected by any outside agency.

Sides and Matches—

SIDE: A player, or two or more players who are partners.

SINGLE: A match in which one plays against another.

THREESOME: A match in which one plays against two, and each side plays one ball.

FOURSOME: A match in which two play against two, and each side plays one ball.

THREE-BALL: A match in which three play against one another, each playing his own ball.

BEST-BALL: A match in which one plays against the better ball of two or the best ball of three players.

FOUR-BALL: A match in which two play their better ball against the better ball of two other players.

Note: In a best-ball or four-ball match, if a partner is absent for reasons satisfactory to the Committee, the remaining member(s) of his side may represent the side.

Slice—For a right-handed player the result of a stroke which gives ball a clockwise spin that arcs its flight to the right of the line from player to objective; for a left-handed player, result of stroke giving ball spin that arcs it to left of line from player to objective.

Stipulated Round—The "stipulated round" consists of playing eighteen holes of the course in their correct sequence, unless otherwise authorized by the Committee.

Stroke—A "stroke" is the forward movement of the club made with the intention of fairly striking at and moving the ball.

Stroke Play (frequently called Medal Play)—Play in which total strokes for the round or rounds determine the winner.

Tee—First, the peg by which the ball is elevated before striking from the teeing ground; second, the teeing ground itself.

Teeing—In "teeing" the ball may be placed on the ground or on sand or other substance in order to raise it off the ground.

Teeing Ground—The "teeing ground" is the starting place for the hole to be played. It is a rectangular area two club-lengths in depth, the front and the sides of which are defined by the outside limits of two markers. A ball is outside the teeing ground when all of it lies outside the stipulated area.

Terms Used in Reckoning—The reckoning of holes is kept by the terms:—so many "holes up" or "all square," and so many "to play."

A side is "dormie" when it is as many holes up as there are holes remaining to be played.

Through the Green—"Through the green" is the whole area of the course except:—

a. Teeing ground and putting green of the hole being played.

b. All hazards on the course.

Top—To hit the ball above its center.

Up—The number of holes or strokes a player is ahead of opponent. See "Down."

1

ORIGIN OF GOLF

Centuries ago, shepherds used to strike pebbles with their crooks, vying with each other in distance and aim. Thus, they discovered, as far as we know, the first game based on hitting a ball with a stick. The game lived and grew . . .

. . . and Caesar's legionnaires brought it to Britain two thousand years ago. It spread throughout ancient Britain in the following centuries until . . .

. . . in the fifteenth century, it was the favorite game of the Scotch. They named it golf. Their equipment was still crude . . .

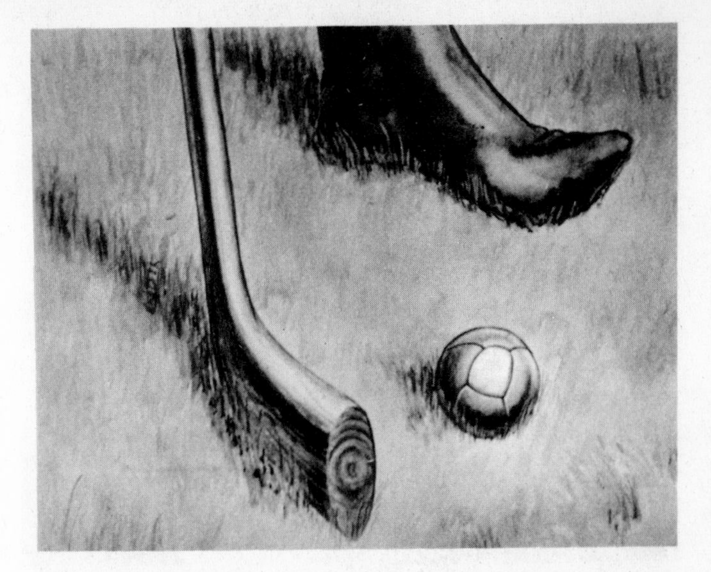

. . . a leather bag stuffed with feathers for a ball and a club cut from a bent tree branch. But, the Scotch enjoyed it so much that, eventually . . .

. . . Parliament declared it illegal. Anyone caught playing golf was fined and imprisoned because Parliament was afraid skill at golf would replace skill with the bow and arrow which was necessary to the defense of the realm.

But, you can't keep a game like golf down. In spite of the ban, the noblemen continued to play in pastures by the sea.

Then, one day, King James IV of Scotland was discovered playing. Of course, from that day on the ban was ignored.

Mary, Queen of Scots, took up the game and became history's first woman golfer. She had an army cadet to carry her clubs . . . hence, the caddies of today. But, even in those days, golf was everybody's game.

In one famous match recorded in this old engraving, a shoemaker, John Pattersone, was partner of King James II, of England, in a match against two noblemen. The king and the cobbler won a sizable bet and the king turned over the purse to Pattersone to build a house. Pattersone called his house "Far and Sure."

With the start of the British Open Championship in 1860, golf got official recognition and this tournament is still held each year.

In America, golf got its impetus in 1880 when a Scot named Reid settled in Yonkers, New York, and introduced it to his neighbors. At first, it was a rich man's game; but its popularity has spread until . . .

. . . today, in America, golf is everybody's game. Six million Americans have made it the nation's favorite outdoor participating sport.

They have found that differences in size, strength and age do not lessen their fun from the game or their ability to play it well.

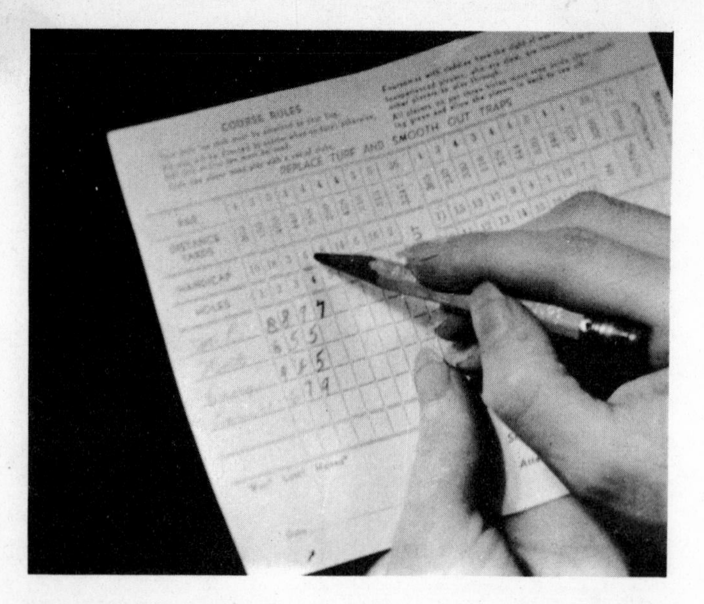

And golf's handicap system adjusts the score so even a beginning golfer can compete with more advanced players with the same challenge and encouragement.

They love the game for its personal challenge. The thrill of achievement is the same regardless of the level of skill.

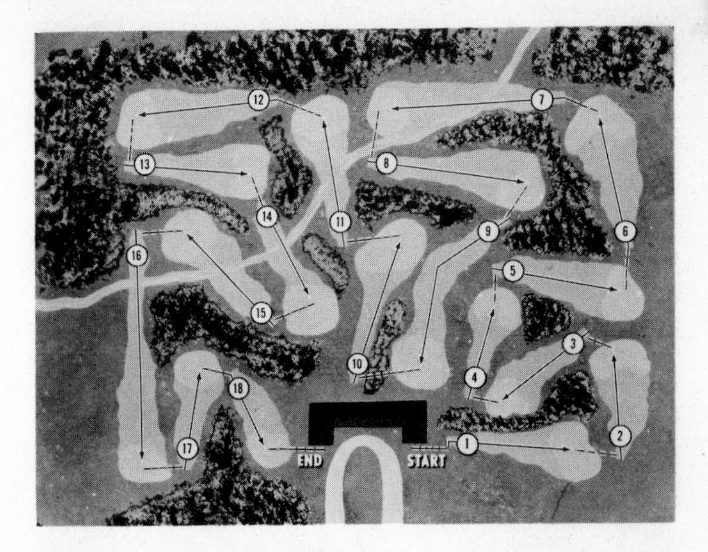

Here is a bird's-eye view of a typical eighteen hole course. Sometimes, where space is limited, a course consists of nine holes. Each hole has a par based on its length. The total of pars for all the holes gives a par for the course. For eighteen holes par ranges in the low 70's. Par, of course, is a standard of excellent play.

And occasionally some golfers enjoy a par-3 course, like this one. The holes are shorter and the game goes faster but the course offers most of the challenges of the standard course and an excellent opportunity to practice.

The starting point of each hole is a tee . . . an area between and behind two markers.

Stretching out in front of the tee is the fairway . . . of close-cut grass flanked by trees and taller grass.

The taller grass at the edge of the fairway is, appropriately, called the rough. There are other obstacles on some holes, too.

Water hazards, like this.

And sand traps, like this.

At the far end of the fairway is the green, a carpet-like area of grass surrounding a cup, marked by a flag.

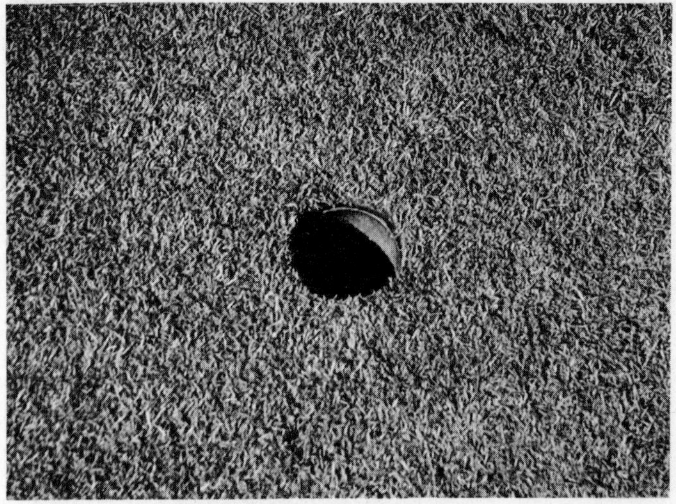

The cup is four and a quarter inches in diameter.

The object of the game is the same on every hole . . . to get the ball from the tee into that four-and-a-quarter-inch cup with as few strokes as possible.

You can select your set of clubs from among many different ones. There are wood clubs for distance and clubs with metal heads—called irons—to be used in various playing situations for controlled flight of the ball.

Among the wood clubs and the iron clubs the chief difference is the angle of the face. They range from nearly perpendicular to a backward slant of more than forty-five degrees. Here's the reason for that.

If you bounce a ball straight against a vertical wall it will bounce straight back at you.

But if you bounce it against a slanted surface it bounces up into the air. That's how you use the slanted faces of your clubs . . . to loft the ball up into the air.

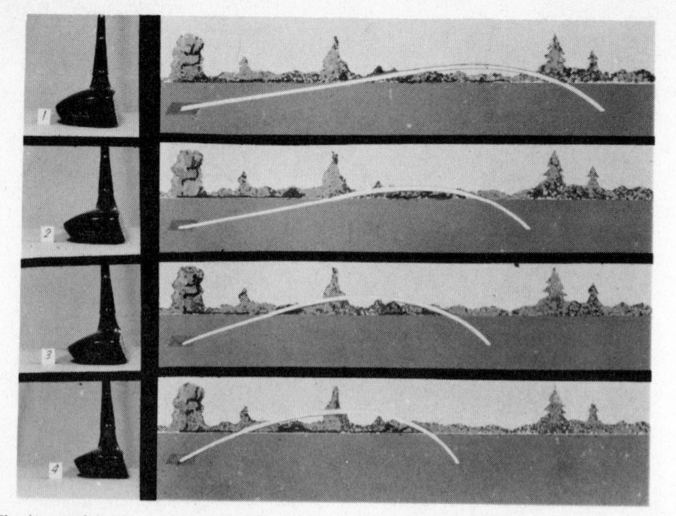

The longer length and less loft of the wood clubs will drive your ball further than the irons. In your basic set of clubs, you'll need at least one of these for long drives . . . probably number one—the driver for shots off the tee . . . and perhaps a number 3 or 4 for long shots on the fairway.

Irons number two and three are called distance or long irons. If you select only one wood club you'll need one of these for long shots from the fairway.

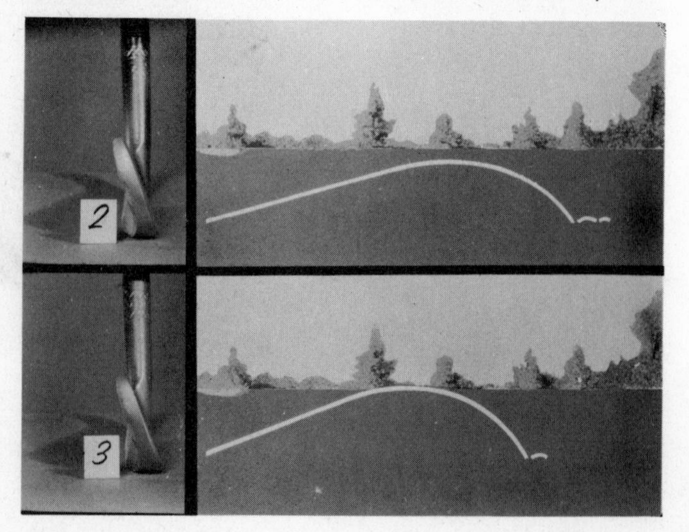

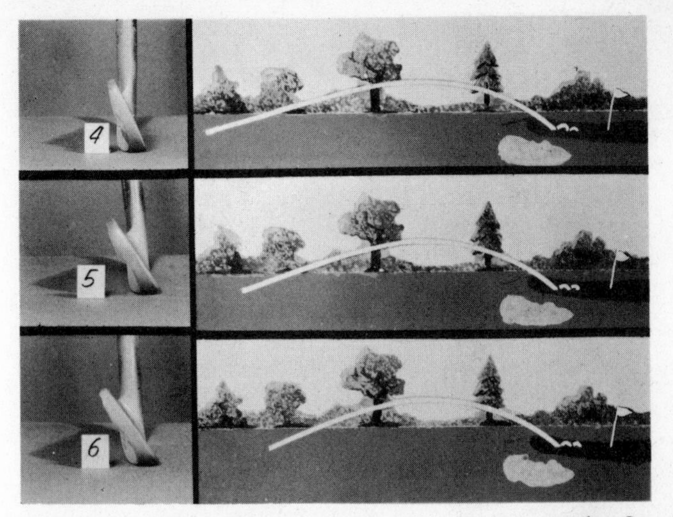

Irons number four, five and six, with their increasingly higher trajectories, are called lofting or middle irons. With them you can hit a ball higher but not so far. One of these is part of your basic set, too.

With number seven, eight and nine, your ball goes even higher; has even less distance, and it will not roll as much on landing. These are called the pitching or short irons. You'll need one or two of these.

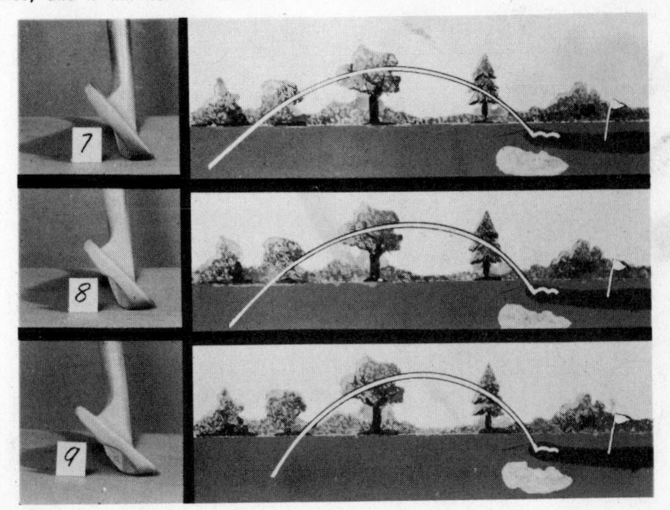

Perhaps you'll want a wedge for shots out of long grass or sand traps. It lifts a ball higher than any other club and shortens its forward roll more than any other club.

And of course you'll need a putter for all shots on the green. The putter, with its straight face, simply rolls the ball along the grass.

So there's all the personal equipment you need to start learning and enjoying golf. For a start, this basic set will handle most playing situations for you. As your skill improves you'll want to add more clubs for more accurate control.

As you learn golf, remember that regardless of equipment, your greatest asset in golf will be your swing. A golf swing is a highly individualized skill and there is much you must know about yourself before you can develop the swing that's best for you.

Your general body type will influence your swing. For instance, how far will you stand from the ball?

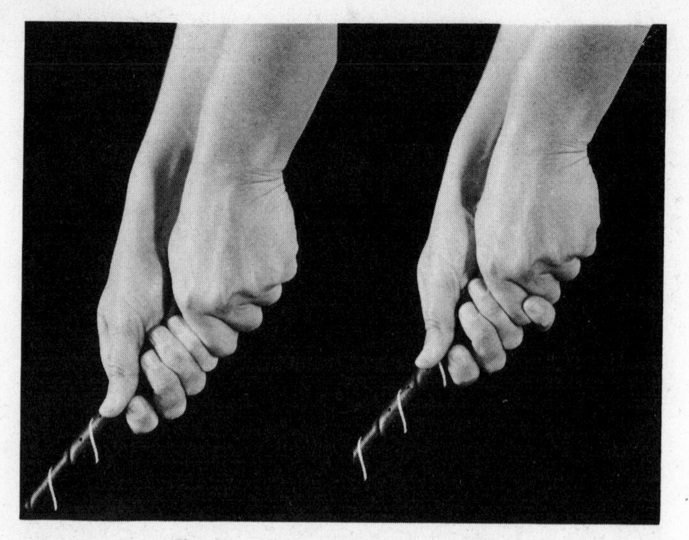

The size of your hands will determine your type of grip.

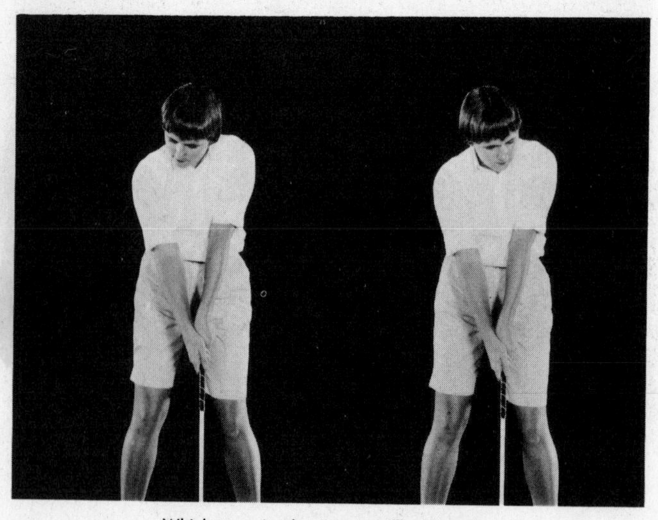

Which eye is dominant, will determine your best head position.

First you'll learn to feel the whole pattern of the swing . . . the oneness of movement . . . the flowing rhythm . . .

. . . of a marvelous system of levers and muscle action that provide the pull and counter-pull of creative and resistive forces.

Then you'll learn the control factors . . . the positions and actions of muscles and joints that work together to give you swing control.

But you'll be ready for fun long before you're satisfied with your swing. As soon as you have any swing at all you can start playing and enjoying it. And all the while you'll keep on learning . . . keep on building control factors into your swing.

2

GRIP, STANCE AND SWING

A good golf game, whether for championship or for the pure pleasure of recreation, is based on a good swing. And there's more to it than just taking a whack at the ball. A good swing must be built.

There is the pattern on which to build it—a graceful swing sequence with three main points—the path of the clubhead, the swing center and the swinging movement.

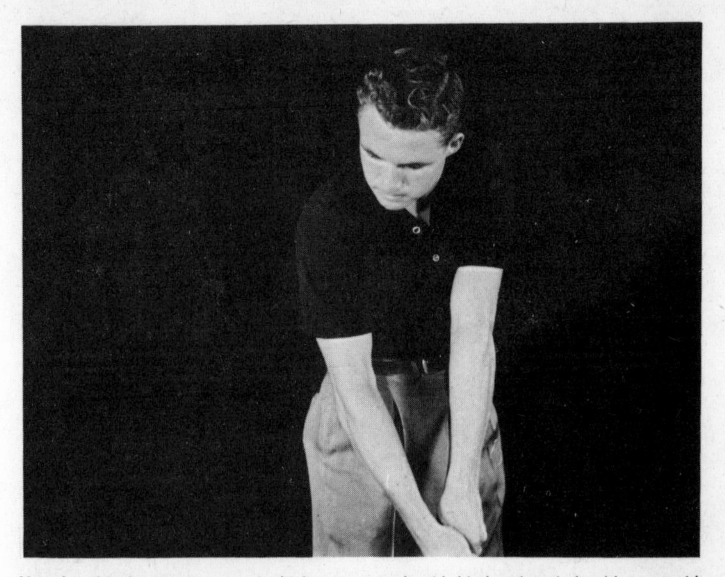

Your head is the center around which your hands and arms swing the golf club. A good golfer keeps himself balanced as much with his head and shoulders as with his feet. Therefore . . .

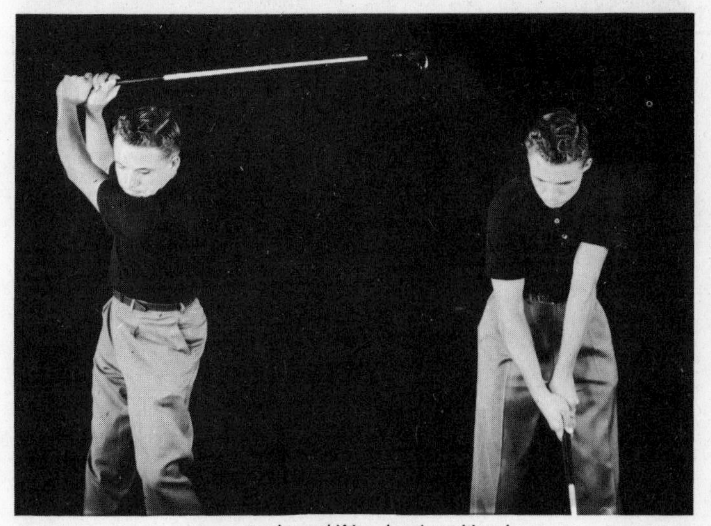

. . . a steady unshifting head position is the axis around which you swing with power and accuracy.

In the backswing the path of the clubhead is a wide sweep in an arc centered on the head.

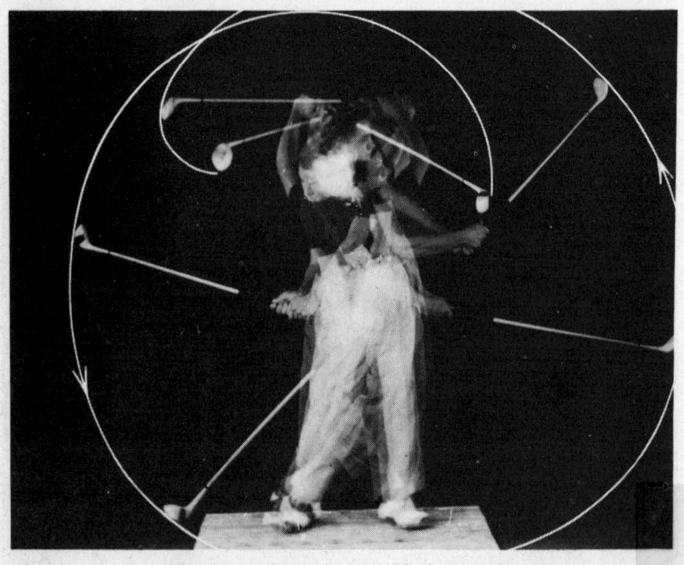

The downswing arc is INSIDE the arc of the backswing. Hand and arm action are coordinated with the body turn in keeping the clubhead on its correct path.

In principle, the club is an extension of your left arm. Your wrists are the hinges between the club and your arms. The hands are the couplings through which power is applied. The security of that coupling depends on your grip.

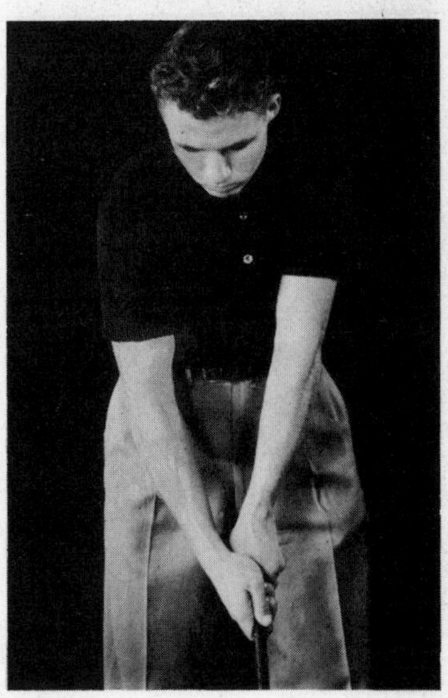

A firm hold on the club—but one that does not stiffen the forearm muscles—is important.

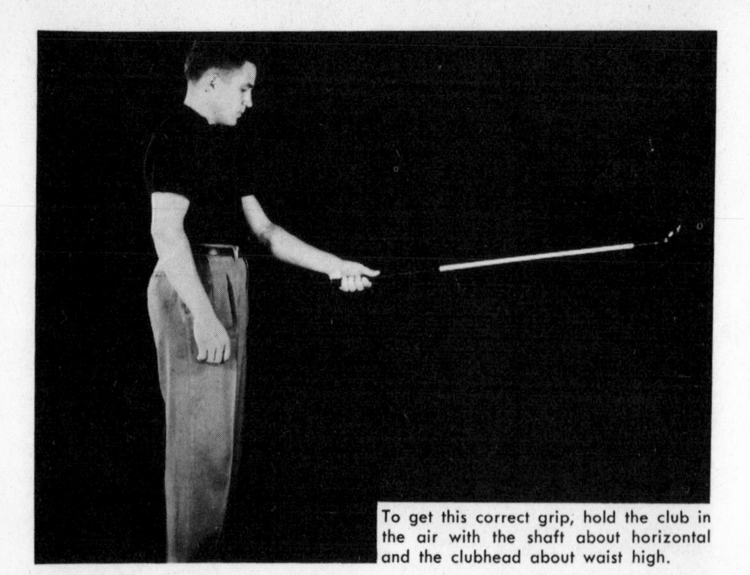

To get this correct grip, hold the club in the air with the shaft about horizontal and the clubhead about waist high.

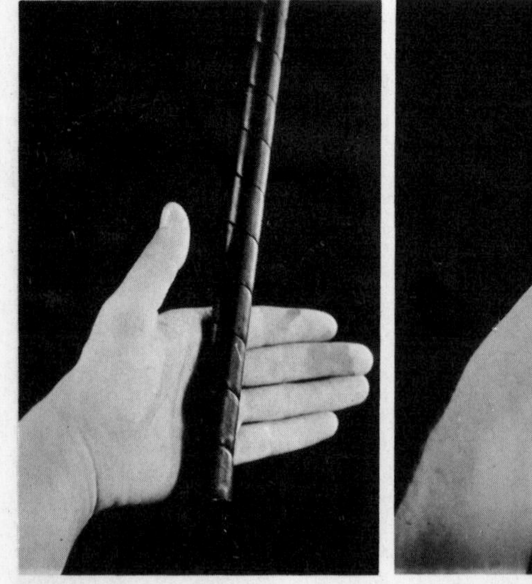

Hold the club in front of you with your right hand and place the shaft across the lower part of your left palm.

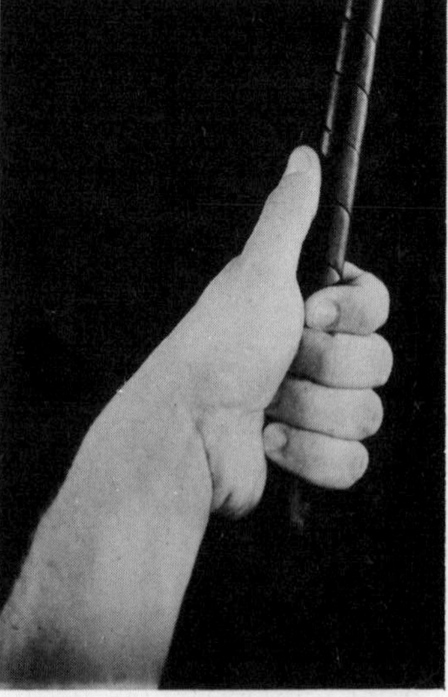

Then grip with your fingers around the shaft, your thumb on the shaft and pointing down.

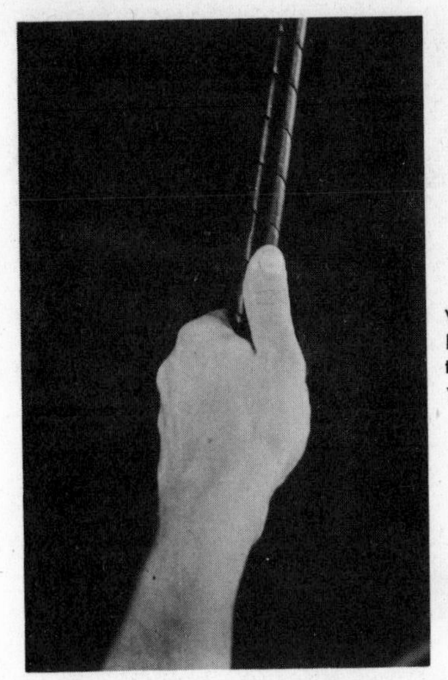

When you turn the club so that the club FACE is perpendicular, the V between thumb and forefinger should point toward your right shoulder.

Here's a check for the left-hand grip. If you hold your club in front of you like this, the last three knuckles should run straight down the shaft.

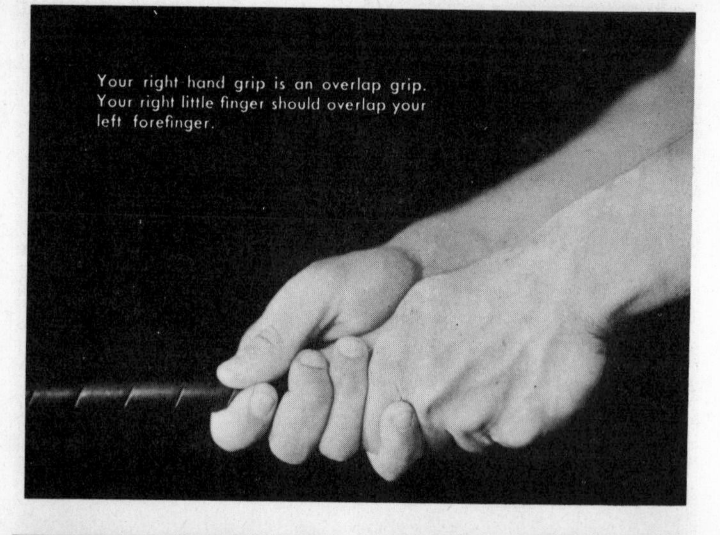
Your right hand grip is an overlap grip. Your right little finger should overlap your left forefinger.

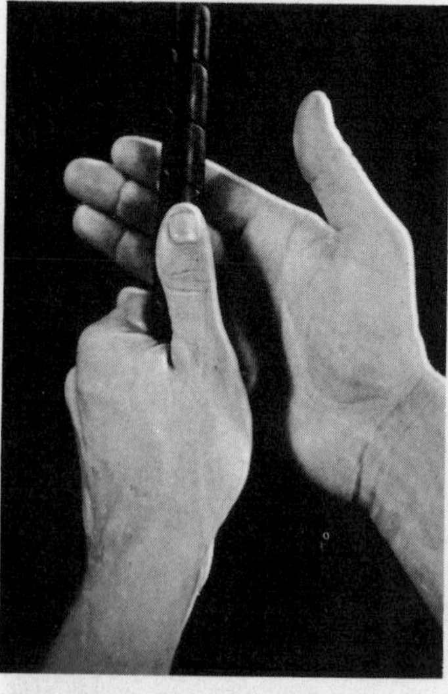
Here's how to get the correct right-hand grip. Bring your hand up alongside the shaft so that your right little finger overlaps around the index finger of your left hand.

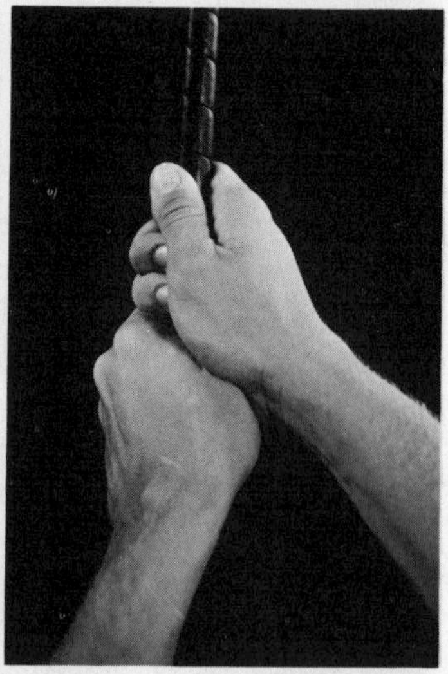
Now close your hand around the club so that your left thumb fits into your right palm along the life line. Your right thumb is around the shaft and meeting the forefinger. The V formed by your right thumb and forefinger also points toward your right shoulder.

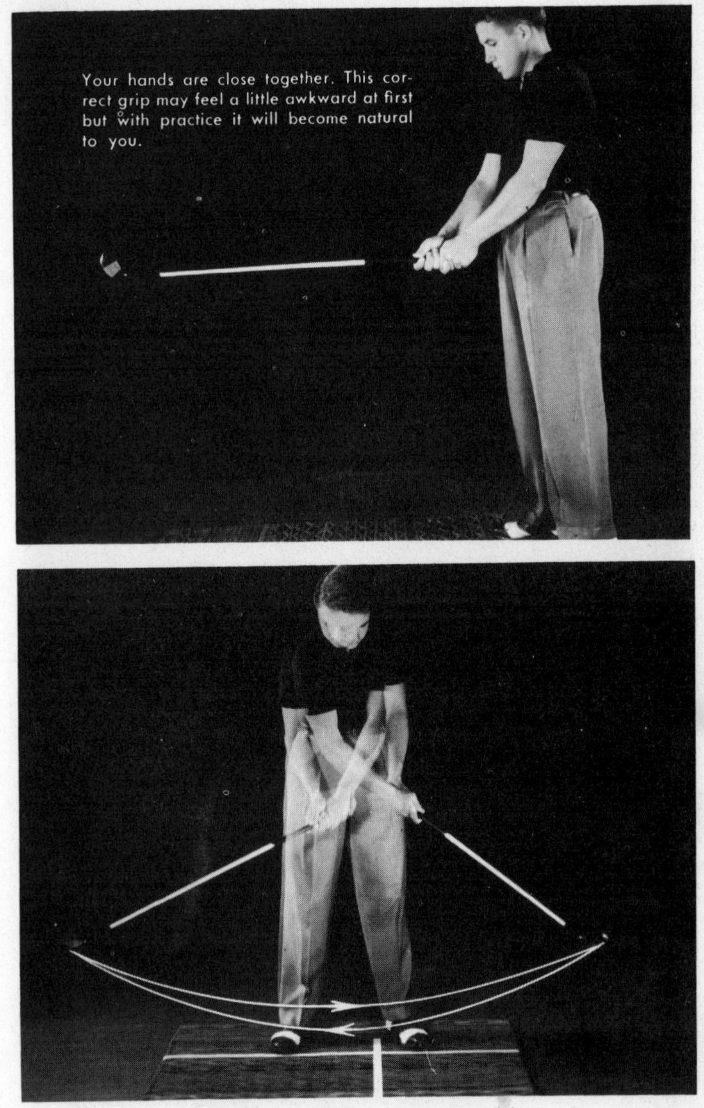

Your hands are close together. This correct grip may feel a little awkward at first but with practice it will become natural to you.

Hold the correct grip and swing your club back and forth a few times to get accustomed to the feel of it. Your left hand is holding firm and your right hand is holding mainly by the fingers.

Starting back from the ball, you feel for your grip as you size up the shot you must make . . . actually plan it and rehearse it in your mind. Then, when all your decisions are made . . .

. . .you move up to the ball. First, put the clubhead down behind the ball, lining up the clubface as nearly as possible to a right angle with the direction you want the ball to go.

Now bring the right foot up into approximate position.

And then the left foot. Through experience and practice, you **feel** these foot positions, approximately.

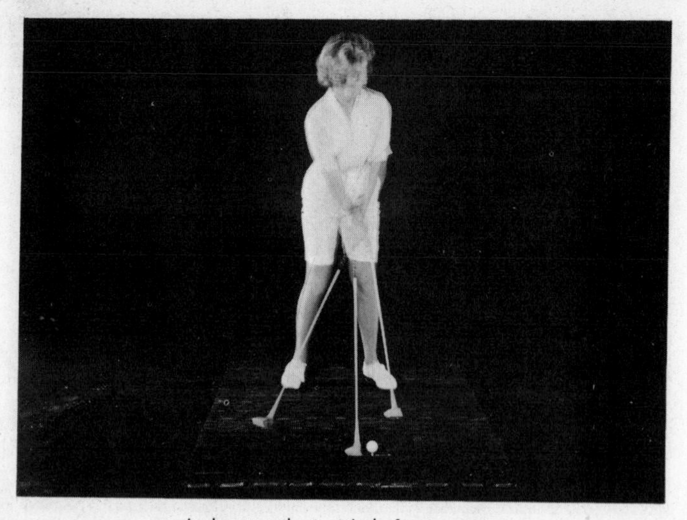

And now a short period of movement as you sight that target again . . . a waggling of the clubhead and a build-up of controlled tension as you put your muscles on stretch. And then . . .

. . . the full swing. A unit move back and then down through the ball position as all your muscles work together in one powerful, controlled movement. This is the swing you will learn.

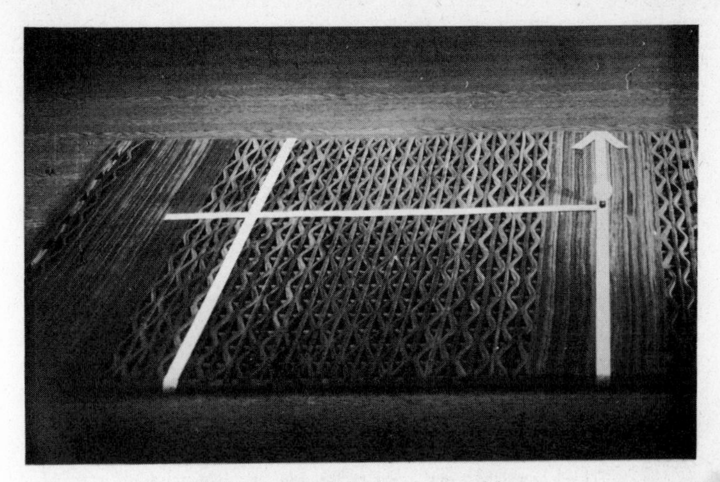

While learning the swing, it is useful to have a stance pattern on the floor. It consists of three lines. . .

. . . one line through the ball in the direction you want the ball to go—this is the direction line . . .

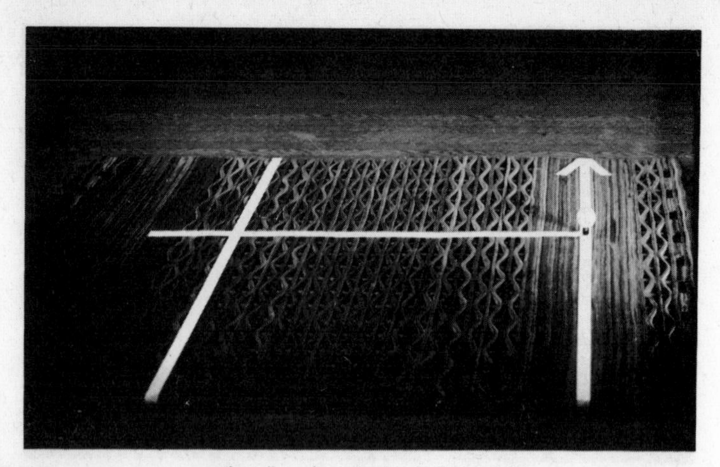

. . . another line through the ball at right angles to the direction line . . .

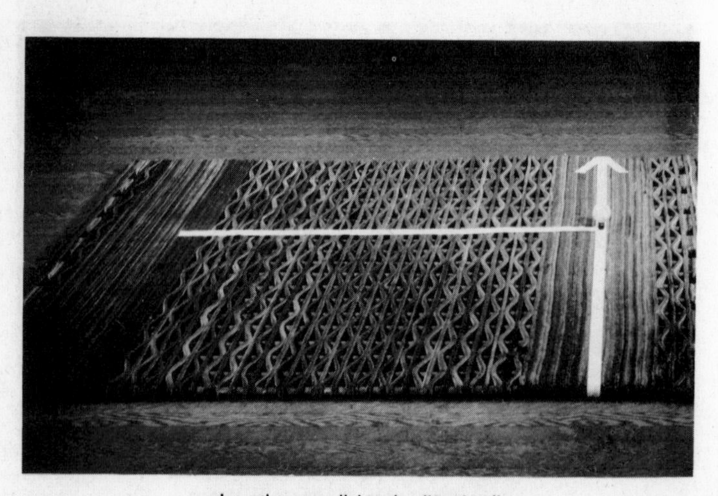

. . . and another, parallel to the direction line, called the foot line.

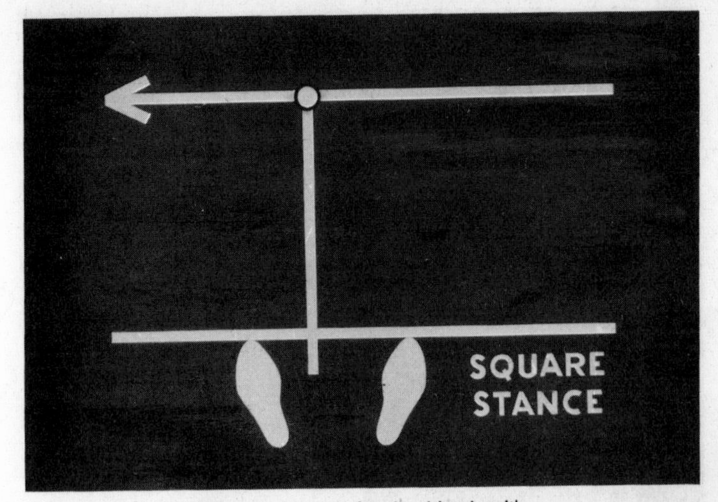

The normal stance for the drive is with your toes lined up square with the foot line. That's called the square stance. Toes are pointed slightly outward. The ball should be an inch or two back of being in line with the left heel.

This is the basic correct posture in this address position. You will have to learn it and make a habit of it.

And there's the correct stance. Ball placement—center to off the left heel. Left foot pointing slightly toward the target . . . right foot square with the master line.

Now for posture . . . your body position as you are ready to swing. It's an attitude of stretch . . . all muscles in controlled tension with an immediate balance sensation.

Your feet should be about shoulder width apart. You'll need this broad base to keep your body balanced and centered during the full swing.

You are aware of your center of gravity . . . that mid-point between head and feet. You're bent at the hips and you feel that your center of gravity has moved back.

Your back is straight . . . so straight it feels as though your seat is sticking out behind. But that's the way it should be.

And your knees are slightly flexed helping to give you that feeling of balance and downward gripping.

Your right knee should be angled slightly inward and you should feel pressure on the insides of the soles of **both** feet. This is most important. You'll need this inward pressure to keep your swing center steady.

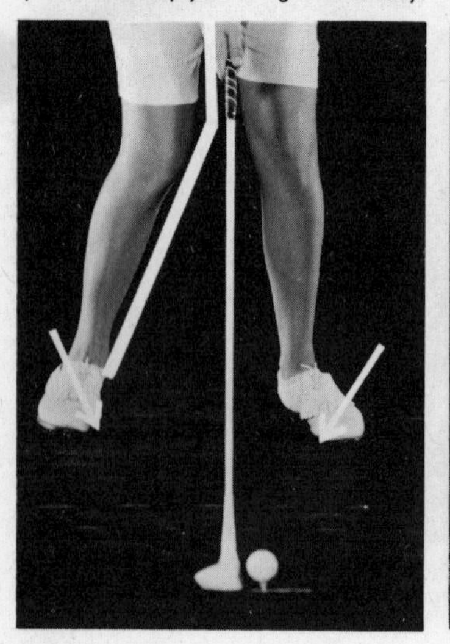

Feel pressure on the insides on the soles of both feet . . . right knee pointing slightly in. In general this is the attitude you will keep throughout the swing.

Most golfers, before hitting the ball, have a preliminary action known as a waggle. It is an introduction, leading into the swing. Just swing the clubhead along the direction line and back. Then place it behind the ball.

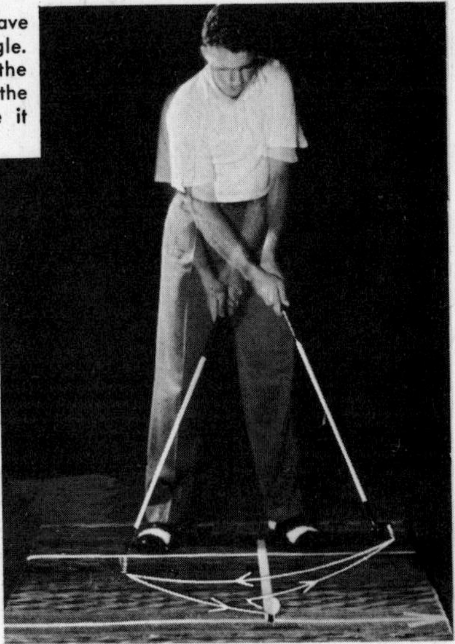

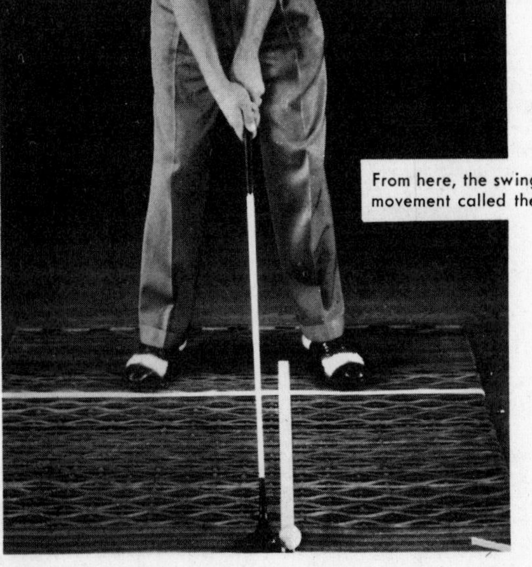

From here, the swing starts with a forward movement called the forward press.

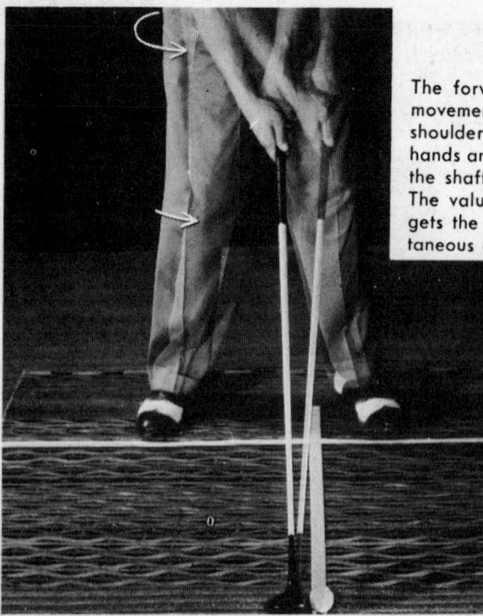

The forward press is a suggestion of a movement of the right knee, hip, and shoulder around to the left that moves the hands an inch or two in front of the ball so the shaft of the club is slanting forward. The value of the forward press is that it gets the body, hands, and arms in simultaneous action easily and smoothly.

The forward press starts the swing movement. Immediately after it, reverse the action of the body twist and start the backswing with an all-together movement of knees, hips, shoulders, arms, hands, and club.

With the hands moving along the foot line, the clubhead is brought back along the direction line, close to the ground, for about two feet. Movement has started in the left knee, hips, and shoulders. The left heel has been raised a little, but the sole of the left foot is still in firm contact with the ground.

At this stage of the swing, the arms do not move independently of the body. Arms and club are being moved by the shoulders—like the spokes of a wheel with the shoulders as the hub.

As the swing continues, the left knee moves forward, lifting the left heel further, but the sole of the left foot maintains a solid grip on the ground.

The left knee moves forward and to the right to a center between the feet. So far, there is very little independent action of the arms and wrists. The angle between the left arm and the club is still approximately the same as in the address position.

Some golfers swing the club almost to the top of the backswing with little or no action in the wrists. Others use the hands freely. A sound medium is to have the club and left arm at a right angle in this position of the backswing.

The body is still winding up and the arms continue on to the top of the backswing with little or no change in the angle between club and left arm.

At the top of the backswing, your body is turned until your shoulders are at right angles to the direction line. Both feet have firm contact with the ground with slightly more pressure on the right. Don't stiffen your right leg. Footwork and the hip and shoulder movement must permit the arms to swing freely.

Your left arm retains its full radius—straight but not stiff. The angle between your left arm and the club is still approximately a right angle. The body has turned and the arms and hands have swung the club until the shaft is approximately horizontal behind the head.

There is the sequence of movement in the backswing—just a winding-up motion that gets you set correctly for delivering controlled power into your downswing.

The downswing is a well-controlled release of this power with your whole body—from feet to finger tips—playing a precise part.

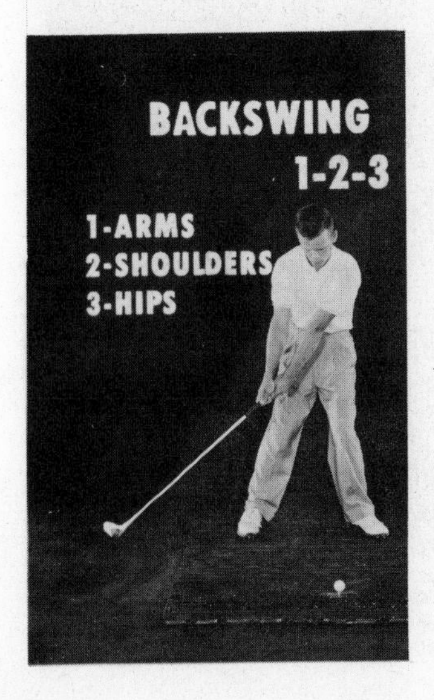

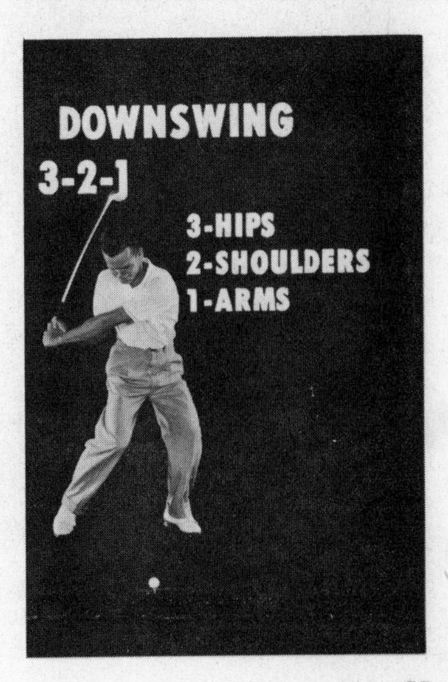

Here is the correct hip angle at the address . . . a bend at the hip joint and a downward feeling in your lower body.

At the top of the backswing the angle at the hip joint is maintained . . . still the upward stretching of the back and the downward feeling in the lower body.

And as you swing into the hitting area the posture is maintained, always keeping your eye on the ball.

It starts in your feet. Your left heel snaps to the ground as your right leg springs, much like a sprinter starting a hundred yard dash. Simultaneously, movement starts in your hips and shoulders.

Here are two views of the springing start, from the top of the backswing, on the left, to the start of the downswing, on the right, as your whole body squares off for the swing.

See how the left side of the body and the left leg are getting into position to be a firm support of the swing. Action of the left and right legs produces a sliding movement of the hips toward the target.

In the early part of the downswing, the right shoulder moves down and the left shoulder moves up as the legs and body come around into the shot. The left leg is slightly bent at the knee but it is firmly supporting the thrust of the right side.

So far, there has been no noticeable movement in the wrists. The shoulders have been forcing the arms down. But just about here, the wrists start to become very active—whipping the clubhead through at greatly increased speed.

When the clubhead hits the ball, it has caught up with the arms and is now practically in a straight line with the left arm from shoulder to ground.

The arms are swinging fast as the ball is hit, but the head and feet have remained firm and steady throughout the swing, providing a solid, unshifting, triangular support for the spine which is the axis of the swing. You hit straight along the direction line.

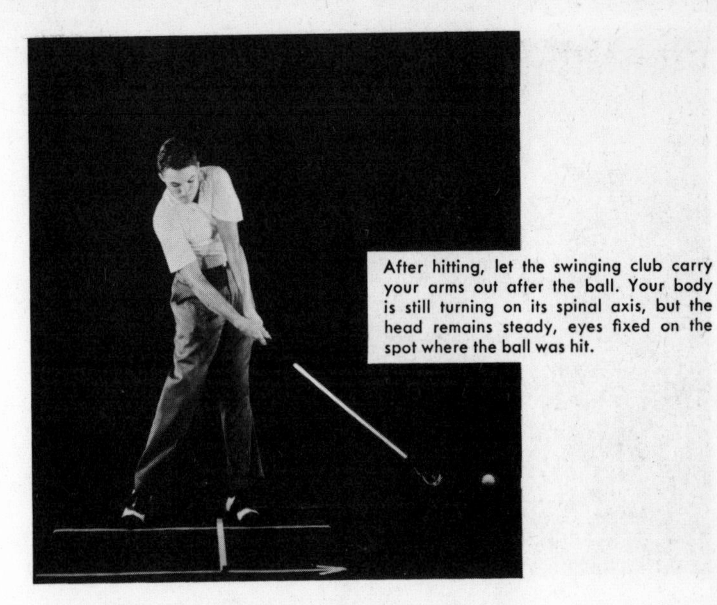

After hitting, let the swinging club carry your arms out after the ball. Your body is still turning on its spinal axis, but the head remains steady, eyes fixed on the spot where the ball was hit.

Only after the ball is well on its way can you let your head turn. Even at this point of the follow-through, it is steady.

Then let your head turn with your shoulders until the club's momentum carries your arms and body around and your weight is all on your left foot.

Your right foot has rolled around until you are on your toes with just enough weight supported on that foot to give you balance. Your head has come up and around naturally.

There's your complete swing. It's a coordinated series of movements made while your feet and head keep you in steady balance. Study the details of the swing; practice them carefully; and very soon, you will build a swing for distance and accuracy that is the true satisfaction of golf.

All the complex movements of a sound golf swing are coordinated into a rhythm pattern . . . a repeatable and very necessary factor in your swing.

Here's the rhythm.

Back and through.
Back and through.

That's the rhythm. Notice how it emphasizes the swing movement.

The "Back" of "back and through" carries you almost to the top of your backswing. It starts back slowly and accelerates smoothly to the top. No jerkiness . . . a smooth flow back and upward.

The "and" emphasizes the direction change for the downswing. There's an almost imperceptible pause for the change of direction of course, but your body is still moving underneath.

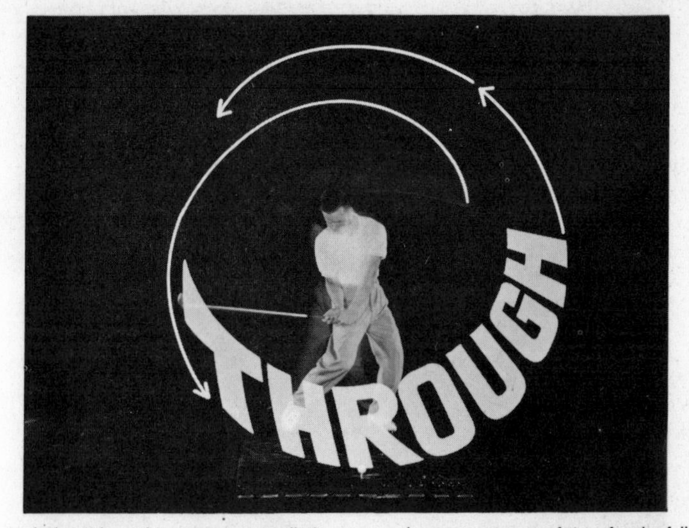

And the "through" carries you all the way from the start of your downswing through the ball to the finish. The swing uses the same amount of time for the full circle of the forward swing as it did for the half circle of the backswing.

Now you try it. And remember, no matter how impatient you may be, the ball will be waiting for you. Don't hurry it. Keep swinging until you can feel the rhythm. It isn't enough to know it. You must **feel** it all through your body.

3

BUILDING CONTROLS INTO YOUR SWING

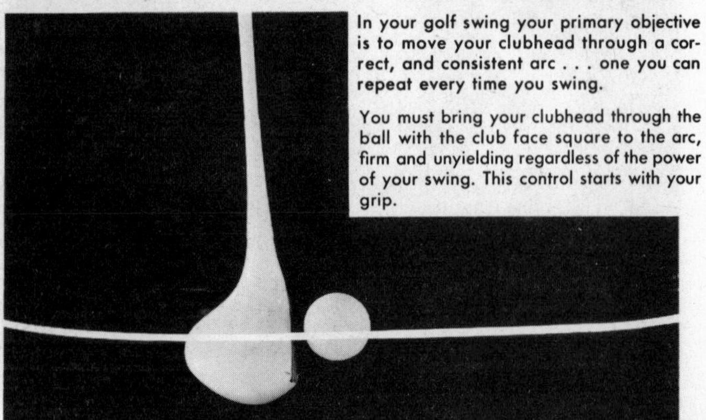

In your golf swing your primary objective is to move your clubhead through a correct, and consistent arc . . . one you can repeat every time you swing.

You must bring your clubhead through the ball with the club face square to the arc, firm and unyielding regardless of the power of your swing. This control starts with your grip.

Your hands must hold the club face square to the intended line of flight and maintain it there throughout the acceleration of the swing. Although the club moves a little in your hand, you must hold on as firmly as you can. This takes strong hands and a correct grip.

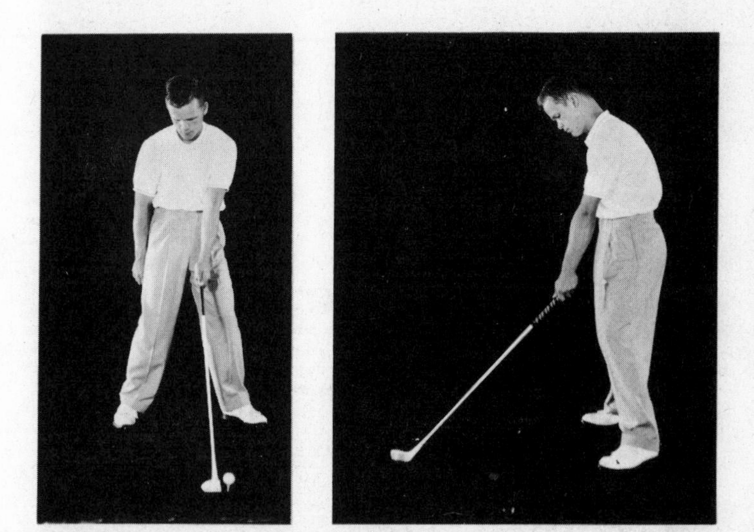

Let's take the left hand first. In a good swing the club shaft seems to be an extension of the left arm. The left hand serves as a firm connector.

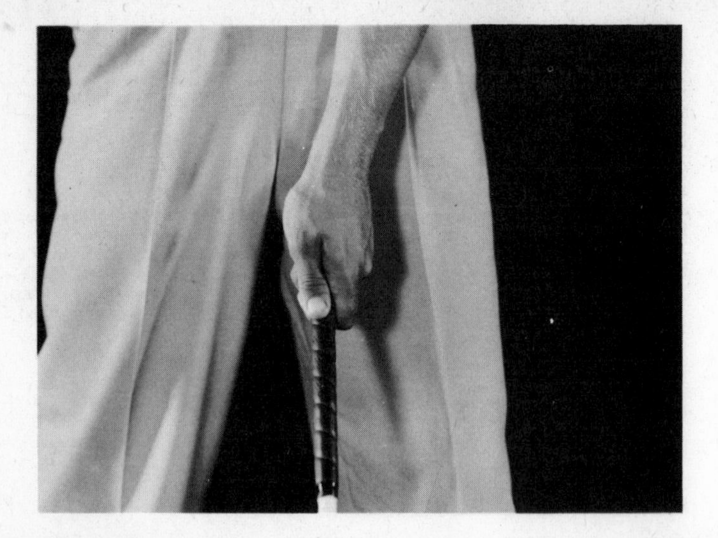

To accomplish this, the club is held down in the fingers of the left hand . . . palm around on top, with the left thumb a little right of center on the shaft. There's a very simple way to achieve this hand position naturally.

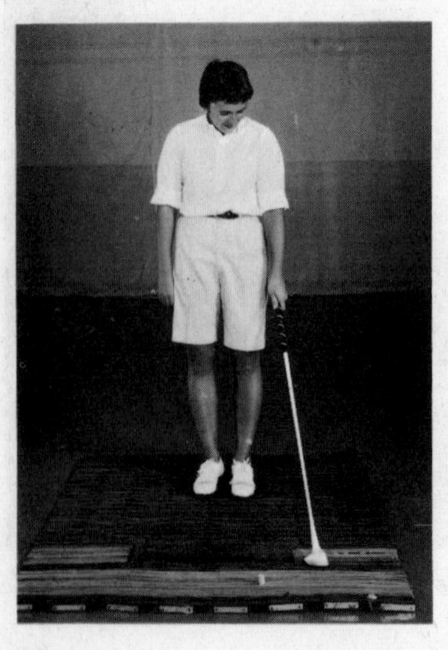

Stand erect with your arm hanging straight down and hold the club off your left side, like this . . . clubhead flat on the ground . . . hand holding the club naturally and firmly, four fingers holding the shaft against the palm of your hand.

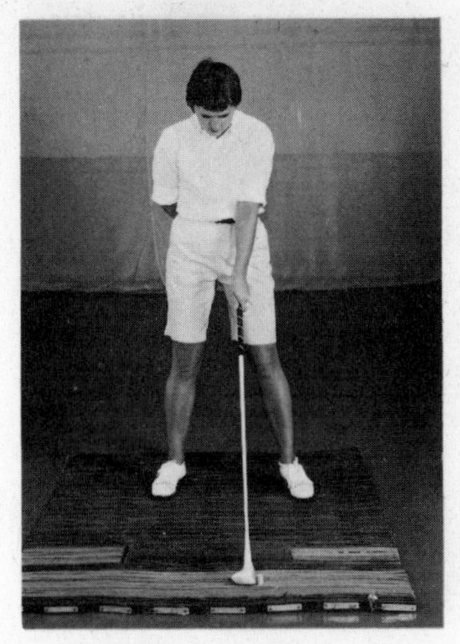

Without changing your hand position, move the club out in front of you and settle into your swing posture.

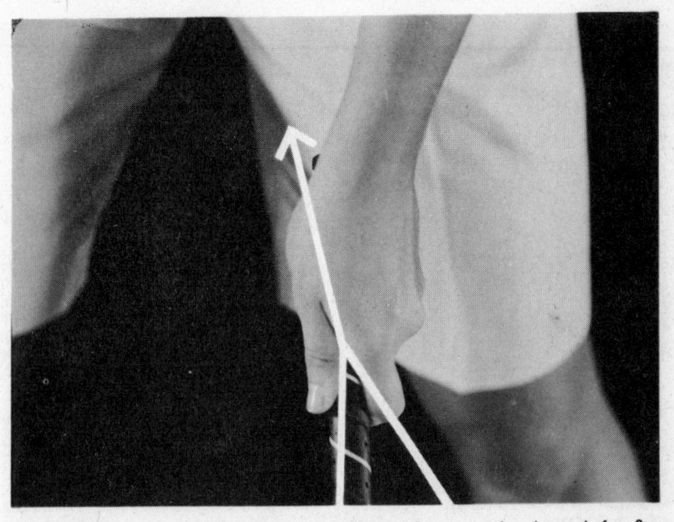

And there's the grip you should have. Make sure the web between thumb and forefinger is closed . . . your thumb pointing straight down the shaft.

The V between thumb and forefinger points to the right of the center of your body.

The real strength of your grip is in these three fingers. You should feel a solid firmness here as they work as a team. They grip into the side of the shaft and press the club against your palm.

If you are a right-handed person, it's going to take time and a lot of practice to develop the strength you'll need in your left hand. But it will come if you swing the club with your left arm only, for a while. Practice this exercise until you start to feel control.

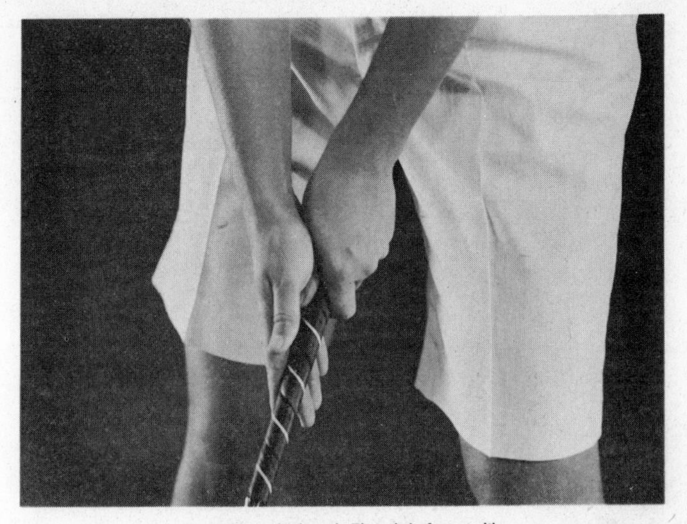

Now the right hand. The club face is like an extension of the right hand. Its action during the swing is like a right-hand slap. So bring it into a slapping position alongside the club shaft.

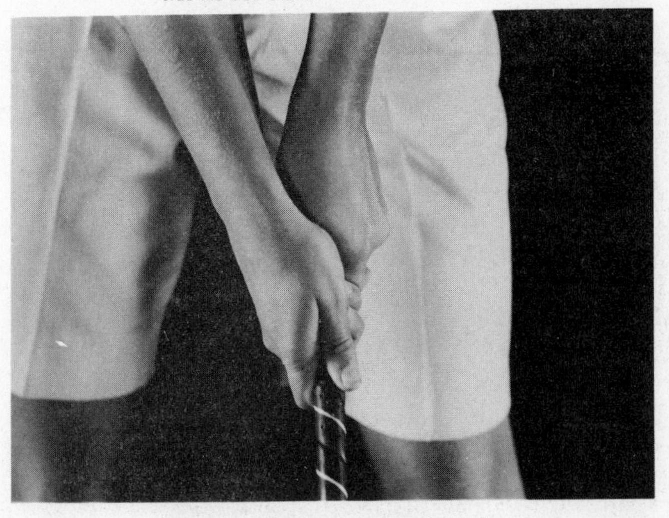

Then just coil the fingers under the shaft, very close and firm against the left hand. And wrap the right palm over your left thumb.

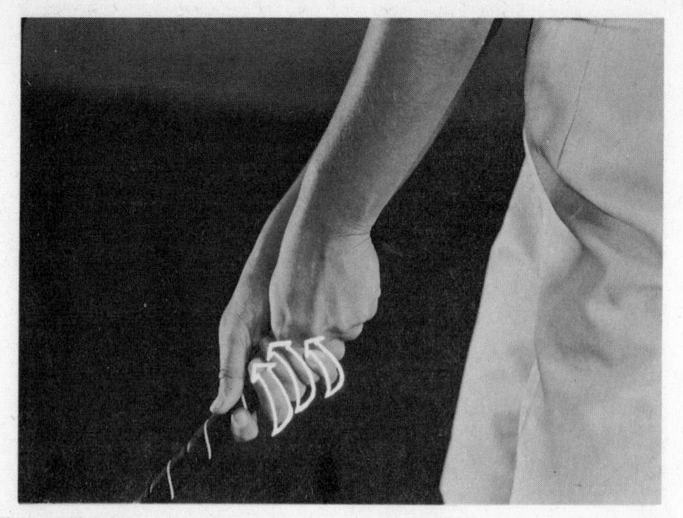

This is called the overlap grip because the little finger of the right hand overlaps the forefinger of the left hand.

You must feel tension in the last three fingers . . . an inward tension as the fingertips press the shaft into your palm.

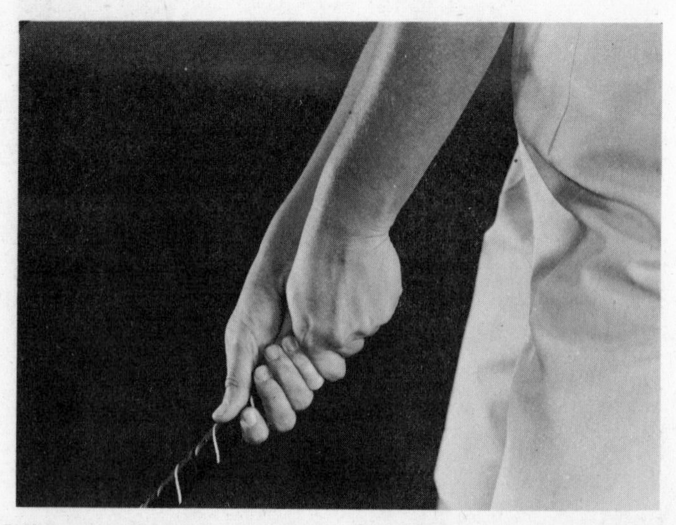

Golfers with small hands or short fingers prefer this four-finger grip . . . all fingers touching the club and the hands pressed firmly together. Others use an interlocking grip by interlocking the right little finger and the left forefinger.

Whichever grip you use, your hands must hold together firmly . . . firmly together and firm on the club. If you relax your grip at all, at any time during your swing, you're bound to lose control of the club face.

That correct and repeating arc through which your clubhead travels during the swing must be carefully controlled, too. And this control is mainly in your arms.

The arc through which your hands move controls the arc through which your clubhead moves. To keep your hand arc constant you must control its radius — your arms.

During your backswing your left arm must be the radius of the arc. For a full, constant arc, it must be extended throughout the backswing.

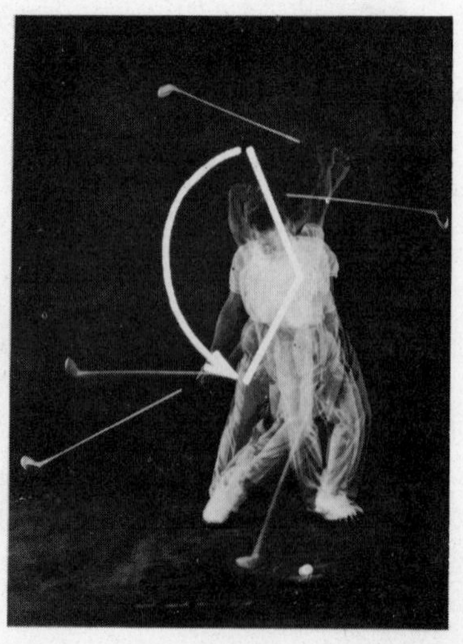

During the downswing, as long as the club is to the right of center, the left arm is the radius of the arc. If you keep it extended, you have control of the arc.

But here, as you swing through the ball position, both arms are the radius. Both are extended.

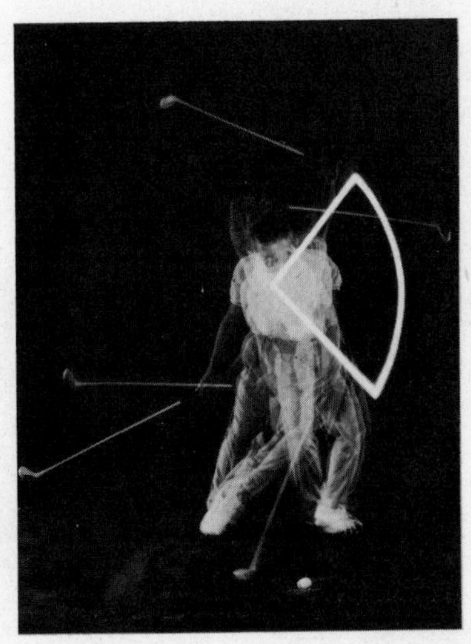

And now, as you roll out into your follow-through, your right arm becomes the radius and it stays extended until the elbow bends naturally.

Obviously, to control the arc of the club-head, you must control the arc of your hands. To control the arc of your hands, you must control the radius. And you keep control by keeping each arm extended when it controls the radius.

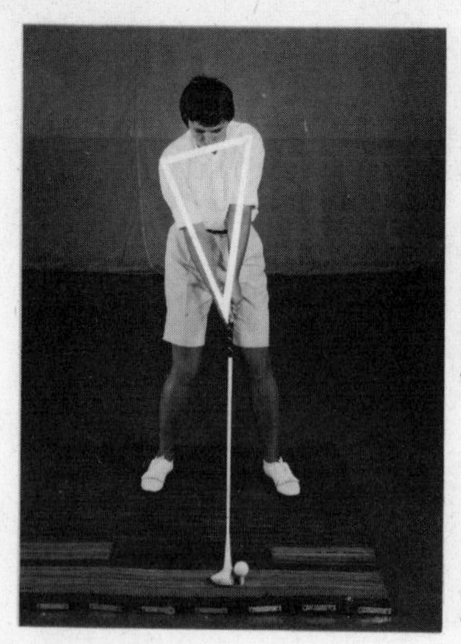

You try it. In your address position, your left arm is extended . . . elbows in . . . right elbow slightly in to your side. Both arms are firm; the grip is secure. An attitude of stretch.

Bear in mind that your shoulders and arms form a triangle and you work to maintain that triangle intact through the swing.

As you start back, club and arms move away as a unit. Left arm extended. Your right arm starts bending at the elbow.

At the top of the backswing your left arm is still extended, right elbow pointing downward. And you keep control of the club face with that sure, firm grip.

During the downswing, keep that left arm straight . . . right elbow still pointing down and moving inward toward the center.

Early in the downswing, your right elbow returns as close as possible to your body and stays there until about here where it starts to straighten.

And as you swing through the ball, both arms are extended, the upper left arm close to the body. But notice the left hand. At this important moment . . .

. . . your left arm is still leading the swing. It's pulling the clubhead through and the back of your hand is well in front of the clubhead.

Now your right arm takes over control of the radius and your left elbow starts to bend. The right arm stays extended until . . .

. . . it bends naturally in your full follow-through.

In summary, here's the arm action. At the address position left arm asserts the control. Part way back, left arm extended, right arm bending. At the top, left arm still extended, right elbow pointing downward.

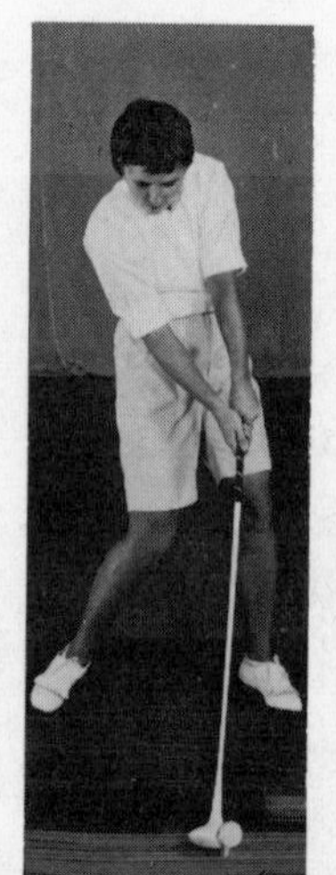

On the downswing, left arm straight, right elbow pointing down and pulling in. At impact, both arms fully extended, left hand leading and pulling. On the follow-through, right arm extended.

Now, to complete the image you should have of yourself as you swing, let's discuss another dimension.

Your stance and posture at address give your swing alignment.

The arc you have habitized gives it extension . . . width.

But your swing has a plane, too . . . the third dimension of a successful swing. It's a round disc, the shape of your swing, from the ball through the juncture of your neck and shoulders and extending behind you. Here's its importance in setting your best angle on the ball.

As you swing back, your clubhead should stay on this plane. Since your club is a straight extension of your left arm, your left arm moves up toward the plane, until . . .

. . . at the top of your backswing, clubhead, shaft and left arm are lined up on the plane. Now you're set at the best angle for your most effective blow at the ball.

As you start your downswing, the angle of the plane changes. It shifts down, inside the backswing plane.

And you swing through on this lower downswing plane with a full circular movement.

Now get set for the whole swing and practice **your** swing some more. Practice until these control factors in your arms and hands become a habit . . . until they feel natural . . . until you have difficulty swinging any other way. Then you'll be ready to think about the power forces in your swing.

The rhythmic speed and coordination of your golf swing results from the interplay of many carefully controlled forces within your body . . . the pull and counter-pull of many muscles. Actually there are very few muscles in your body that are not involved in your golf swing.

To understand the interplay of muscles during a swing let's analyze the creative forces first . . . but bear in mind that all through the swing the resistance forces are exerting the counter-pull necessary to keep the spinal axis steady.

Think of yourself as a system of levers—your bones—operated by a system of springs—your muscles.
Your club and your arms are a single interlocking unit—the radius of your swing arc.
In the region of your spine is a vertical axis. Your shoulders and arms revolve around it.

Your hips are a turning lever at the other end of the spinal axis. To operate this lever system in your golf swing and generate power for the swing you use three sets of muscles in your upper body.

The large muscles in your waist and thighs give power to your hip movement.

The powerful muscles in your back add more power through your shoulders.

And the big muscles in your shoulders and upper arms build the power further by pulling your arms around.

As you get set to swing, your muscles are on stretch . . . a controlled tension . . . and the first movement of the backswing involves muscles all through your body. The pull and counter-pull through all your muscles starts when the swing starts. But, for now, let's think only of the sequence of major muscle movements during the winding and unleashing of the swing.

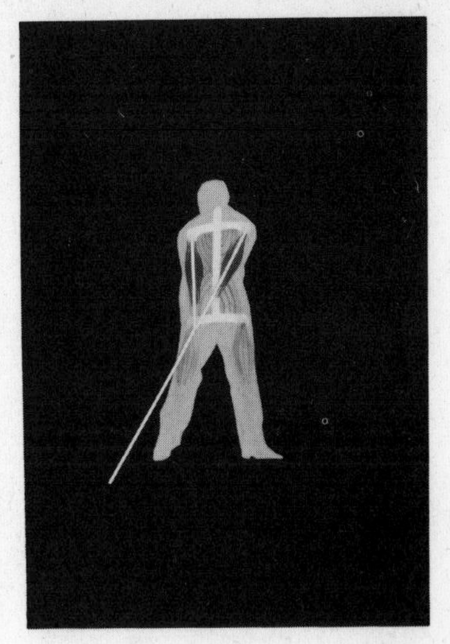

The first conscious increase in muscle tension is in the arm and shoulder muscles. They start the radius rotating around the axis . . . a winding-up movement. So far, back and thigh muscles haven't come into conscious play.

But here the shoulder and back muscles continue the turn.

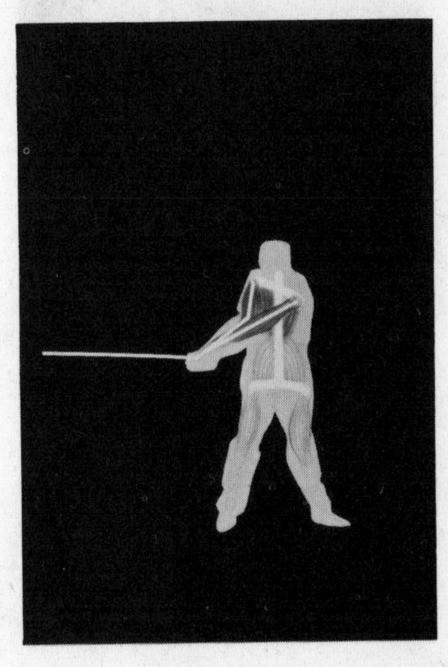

And finally, your waist and thigh muscles come into conscious play and the turning movement is complete.
From above, here's what you should feel like. A powerful set of springs, all wound up and ready to unwind with tremendous power . . . power held in check by the resistance forces in your lower body.

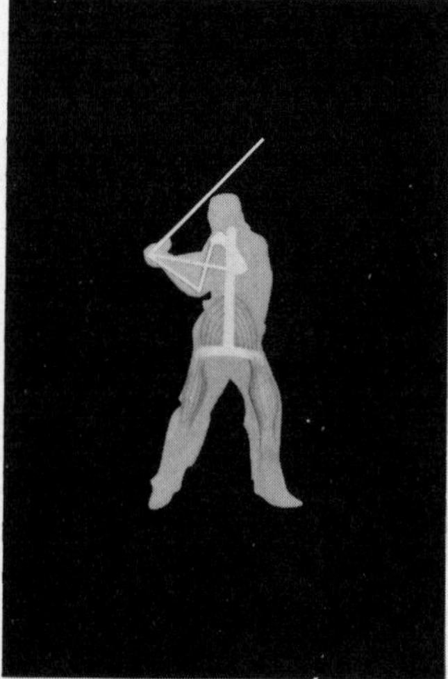

In the downswing, the first application of major power is in your hip area . . . a powerful pull around the steady spinal axis.

Immediately, the back muscles pick up the progression of power and turn your shoulders. Power is building up now . . . thighs, hips and back muscles working together.

And then, in smooth progression, your shoulder and upper arm muscles join the power team and, all working together, they pull the arms and clubhead through.

There's the sequence of creative forces. Arms, shoulders, hips on the winding backswing. Hips, shoulders, arms, on the unwinding downswing. Arms, shoulders,

hips—hips, shoulders, arms—1, 2, 3—3, 2, 1. Now what about the resistive forces? What about staying centered?

Remember Newton's law: "For every force there must be an equal and opposite force." That's the law that works to keep you centered in your repeating swing.

During the backswing there is a mild swing force to the right. This is balanced by . . .

. . . an equal and opposite resistive force through your right foot. Your right knee points slightly inward, ready to increase that force as the swing builds up its potential power.

As you start down in the downswing the swing force builds up quickly and powerfully to the left. But simultaneously . . .

. . . your right leg sets up an equal and opposite resistive force to keep you centered. Your right foot is digging in to keep that swing center steady.

As you swing through the ball, swing force is strongly forward.

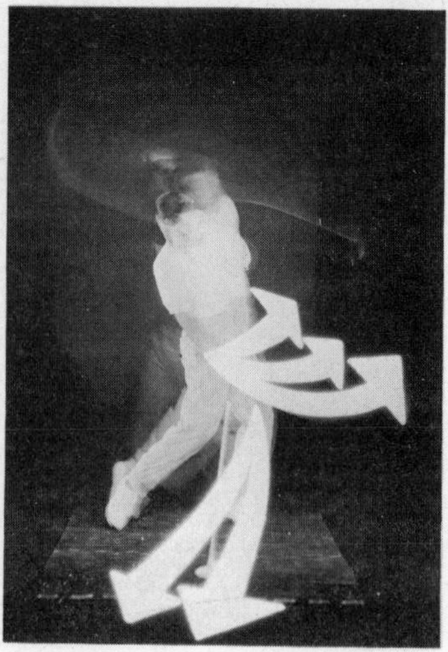

And now a strong bracing action down your left side provides the resistance.

Now you and your club are pulled upward and you come to rest in static balance with most of your weight on your left foot.

Here is the critical point — you change direction. From here you build up speed and keep going. You form into center before you let the arc expand. And, really, from this point on there is no conscious control.

Speed is still building. You're thinking through the ball. You're planning on a long flat through the ball. You've got to accelerate and you've got to hold on.

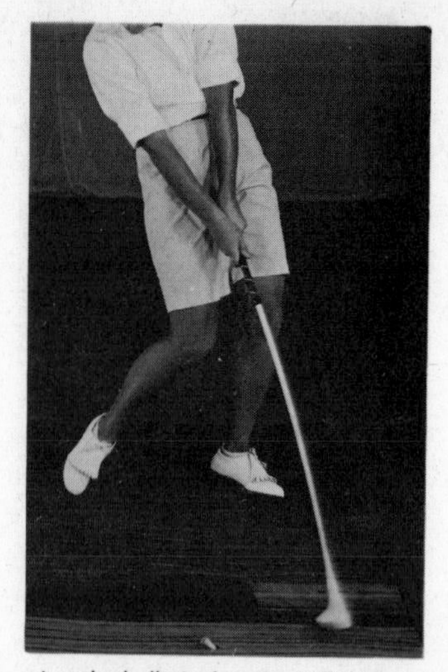

You're still thinking through the ball . . . power is coming from your trunk . . . your hands merely holding the club face against the ball. And you're still trying to accelerate through the ball.

There's no letup here . . . no collapse of the swing. Notice the long extension of the arms.

And the roll-out. Your feet have resisted and reacted. Throughout the swing they have resisted but they have been pulled along by the swing. You have not purposely moved them. And now, temporarily poised and balanced, you make a quick review of your swing . . . replay it for yourself. How did I do? What can I do better?

The carefully controlled, repeating swing you build is only a part of the complete golfing movement. In addition to this, you will need a routine approach to the ball that should precede every swing.

It starts well behind the ball. Here you plan the shot you must make. You are planning so carefully that you can actually feel the swing before you make it . . . a kind of mental rehearsal. Then, when all your decisions are made . . .

. . . you move up to the ball, first grounding the club behind it and setting the shaft as nearly as possible to a right angle with the line to the target.

Then place the right foot into approximately the position for your stance. Placing the right foot first keeps you facing the target and helps you to aim.

Then the left foot up into position.

And now a short period of preliminary motion as you get set to swing. You shift your feet, adjusting your balance; sight the target again and make sure your body is lined up. Meanwhile, your club is moving behind the ball. Your muscles are on stretch and you're getting ready to swing. And then . . .

. . . all the control factors you've learned and habitized come naturally into your swing. You don't think about them. If you've practiced well enough, they're there.

4

GETTING ONTO THE GREEN

When your ball lies in the fairway grass and you can't just roll the ball toward the cup . . . you have a completely different problem and you must call on a different skill.

Now you must stroke the ball so it will travel through the air over the fairway grass and land on the green with enough roll to get it within good putting distance of the cup. This is called a pitch-and-run shot . . . sometimes a chip shot.

It can be done successfully from the edge of the green . . .

. . . or from far out on the fairway. Depending on your skill and power. Near or far . . . short shot or long . . . the basic fundamentals of the pitch-and-run shot are the same.

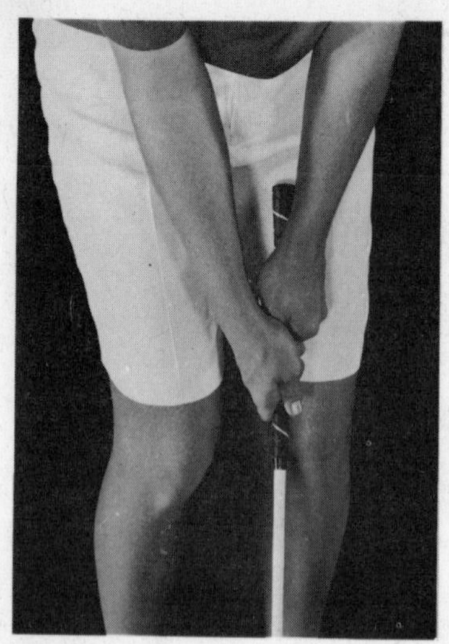

Let's analyze the shot for very short distances first.

Posture is the same as the familiar golfing posture . . . body bent at the hips, knees flexed, a feeling of settling down over the ball. You're close to the ball because . . .

. . . the club is shorter and you grip further down on the club for this short shot.

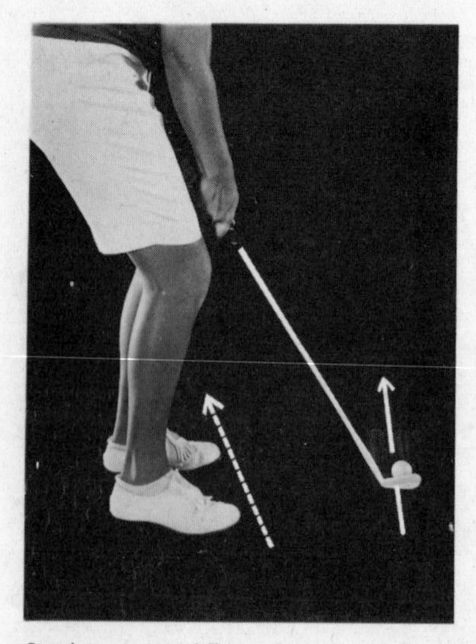

But the stance is different from that of the full swing. Your feet are closer together and the left foot is drawn back a little and it points slightly more toward the hole. The weight is slightly heavier on the left foot. The ball is played off the left heel.

There is the complete movement for very short pitch-and-run shots. Backswing and follow-through just about equal in length. The club pointing downward at the end of the shot. But, and this is important, notice the steadiness of the body. It has not moved noticeably throughout the swing. Instead, movement is in the arms and hands. The move is a pulling action and resistance in your feet gives you something to pull against.

During the backswing, the clubhead starts as close as possible along the direction line, club face always square to the line. The right elbow hinges.

Throughout the swing, the wrists are firm as you move the club forward along the direction line.

You stroke the ball crisply, wrists stay firm, the back of the left hand leading the movement. In this short shot, the left hand leads and pulls, the right hand swings through.

And at the end of your follow-through your left hand has still not relinquished its leadership. You end the shot with a low follow-through.

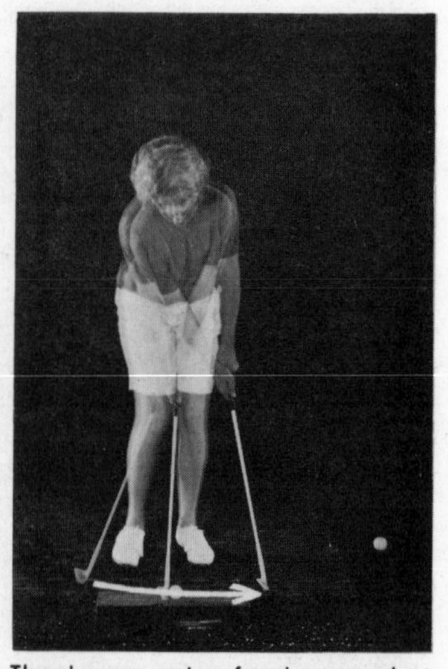

There's your swing for the very short pitch-and-run shots; those critical chip shots from just off the green. Practice it until it works for you . . .

. . . until you can make the ball travel through the air over the fairway grass; land on the green, and roll close to the cup.

Then practice it from steadily increasing distances away from the green.

The longer shot is basically the same . . . simply longer and stronger. The same left hand control; the same crisp movement; the same follow-through with the weight of the club down. But a little wider stance; a little longer backswing, with the right elbow hinging and a little longer follow-through.

The swing gradually increases in length and strength until ‘rom well out in the fairway, say about thirty yards, it will look like this.

Skill with your pitch-and-run swing will save you many strokes around the green where control of both distance and direction become so important.

But there will be times when you won't want the ball to roll so much on the green. Here, for instance, you would want to . . .

. . . make it travel through the air over the fairway grass and the trap and land on the green with very little roll. Otherwise it would roll well beyond the cup. You can do this with a pitch shot.

Here's the basic difference between the pitch-and-run shot and the pitch shot. In the pitch-and-run shot your ball travels about one-third of the distance through the air and rolls about two-thirds of the distance. In the pitch shot, the trajectory is higher; the ball travels about one-third of the distance through the air and rolls a much shorter distance.

Here's your pitching swing that will give your ball the high flight you need to drop it on the green with very little roll. Basically, it's the same as your pitch-and-run swing; but there are these important differences.

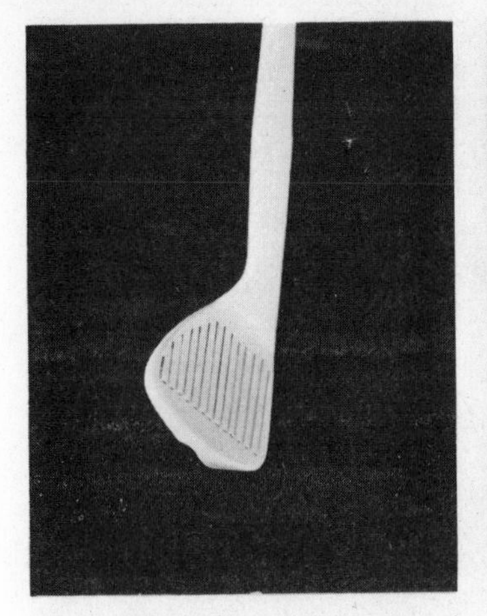

Use the most lofted club you have . . . if not a wedge, then at least a nine iron.

In the backswing, you let the clubhead swing back further, with the right elbow hinging, causing your wrists to break slightly.

Your downswing is not quite so crisp . . . more of a swing. But your left hand still leads; your left wrist still holds firm . . .

. . . and as you follow through, the clubhead swings on through further.

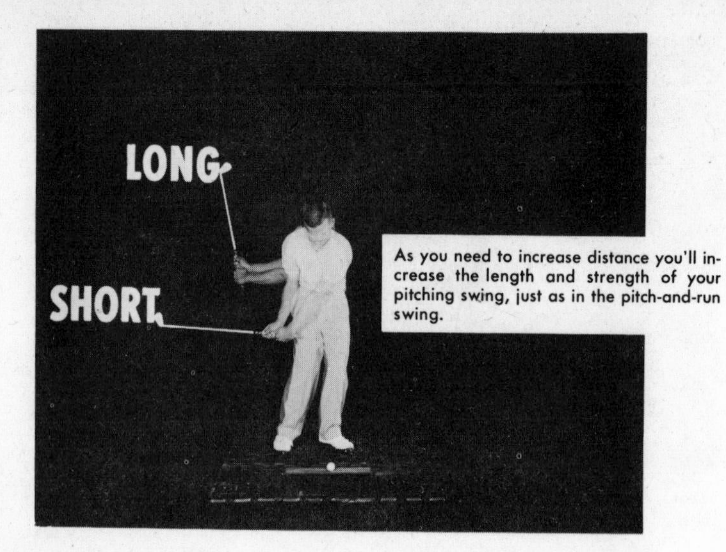

As you need to increase distance you'll increase the length and strength of your pitching swing, just as in the pitch-and-run swing.

It's a natural lengthening, taking on more and more of the character of the basic full swing as distance increases.

Hitting a ball out of sand requires a different club and a slightly different swing.

But it can be a really thrilling shot. It's called an explosion shot.

Your sand wedge, the club you use for explosion shots, has a flat, broad base to bounce its way through the sand without digging too deep.

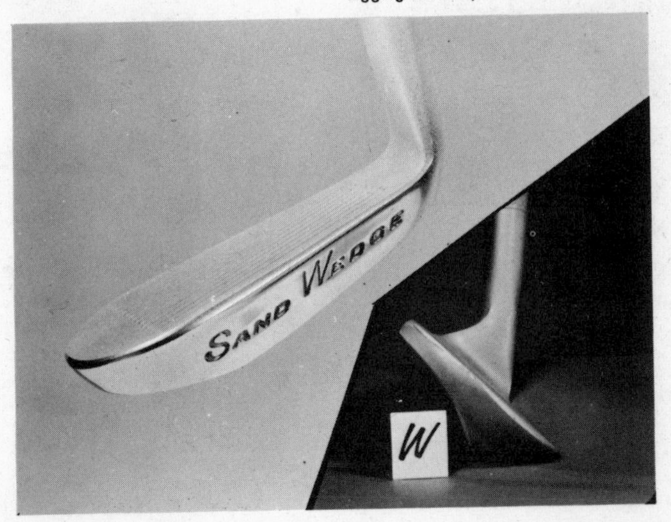

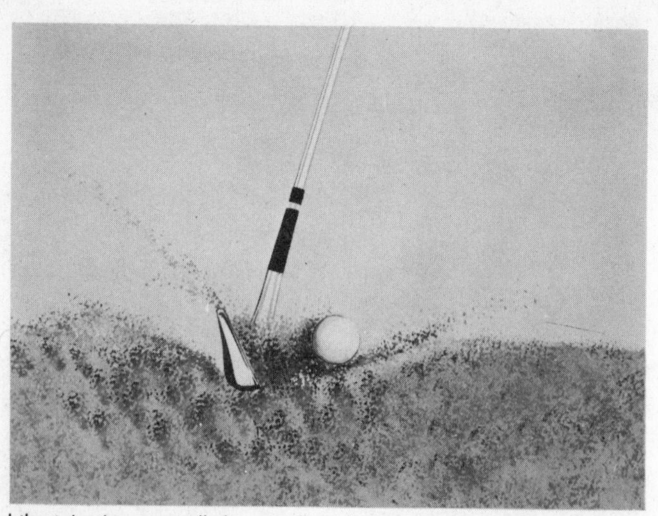

And the swing is so controlled as to pull the clubhead through the sand under the ball and let the compression of the sand pop the ball up toward the target. Actually, the club face doesn't touch the ball. Compression of the sand transfers the swing force to the ball.

Your explosion swing is exactly like your pitching swing with three important differences.

As you address the ball for your pitching swing, as on the left, you set your club face square to the direction line. But for an explosion shot, as on the right, you open the club face . . . angle it back slightly. This gives your ball a high flight.

Your explosion swing is more upright. You start the clubhead back at an angle outside the line of flight and hold it in that plane through the backswing. And you bring it back down through the same arc on the downswing, cutting slightly across the direction line as you swing through the ball position.

In your explosion swing you don't hit the ball directly. You pick a spot an inch or two behind the ball and actually hit into the sand.

You must get the ball up and out. With that in mind, you must finish your swing. Pull the clubhead through the sand.

An important part of golf skill is your play with your distance irons and the shorter irons for hitting the ball higher into the air. Your swing with these clubs is basically the same as with the wood clubs. The stance, however, is different.

For long shots with your irons, your feet are a little closer together and closer to the direction line.

In the address of iron shots, your hands are more in front of the ball than with wood clubs.

The swing is exactly the same as with the wood clubs except that you don't go quite as far back on the backswing. Also, the fact that your hands are a little ahead of the clubhead on the swing makes the lowest part of the arc of your swing a little ahead of the ball. You hit down on the ball and take a little turf after hitting.

In the address for medium iron shots notice that your feet are a little closer to the ball than in the address for the longer iron shots.

And your swing is basically the same—just shortened on the backswing and at the end of the follow-through.

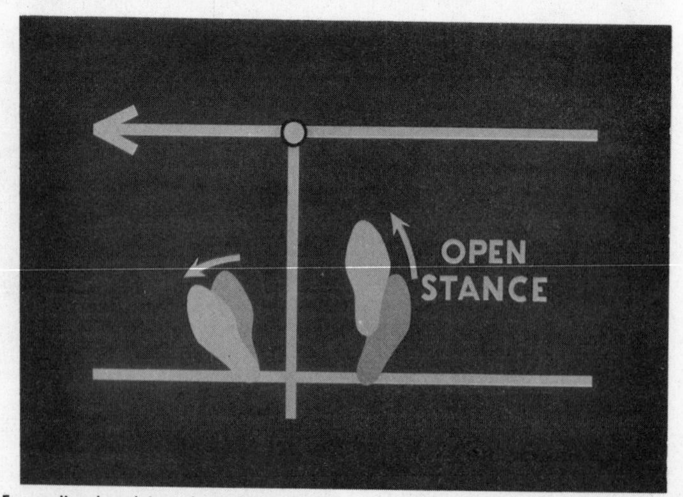

For medium-length iron shots of about 100 yards or less, with the lofting clubs, you use what is called an open stance which turns you slightly toward the hole. Your right foot is closer to the ball. The open stance keeps the arms closer to the body and reduces the tendency to allow too much body turn.

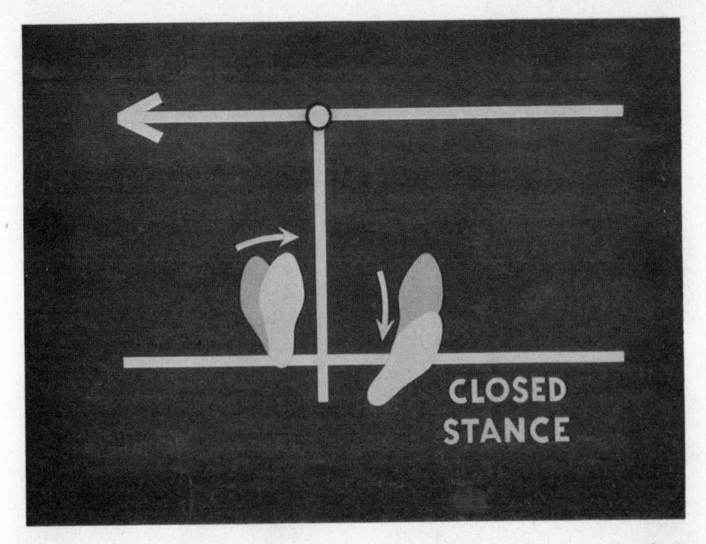

A closed stance is when the left foot is closer to the direction line than the right foot is. It makes it easier for some players to turn the body. Generally, the shorter the shot to be made, the closer together are the feet.

For the short iron shots, you move a little closer to the ball and have your feet closer together.

5

PUTTING

When you get your ball on the green, you must bring a new golf swing into play. Putting is different. And putting is individual.

Watch the players on any putting course and you'll see as many different putting techniques as there are golfers putting. And most of them are effective.

Among the consistently good putters you'll see certain fundamentals they all use, regardless of variations. If you follow these fundamentals you'll find success.

In the address position, you are bent over from the waist, knees slightly flexed. You feel centered over the ball.

Your eyes are directly over the ball.

There's your address position. Study it carefully. Your weight is mostly on your left foot . . . right foot balancing. You should feel your grip on the ground on the inside of the soles of both feet, a somewhat knock-kneed feeling of inward containment.

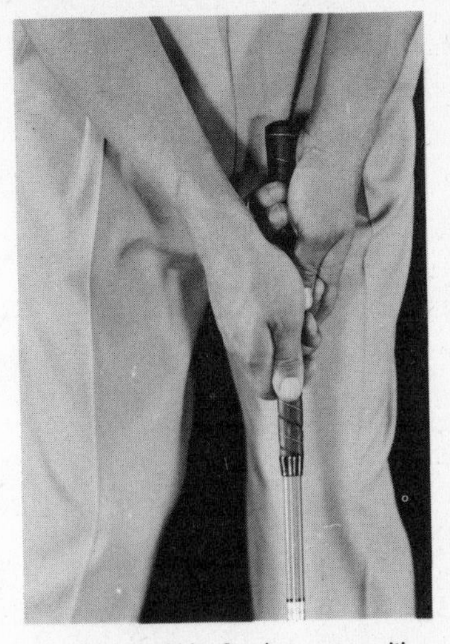

Your grip should be firm but very sensitive. Don't squeeze. Both thumbs are straight down the shaft.

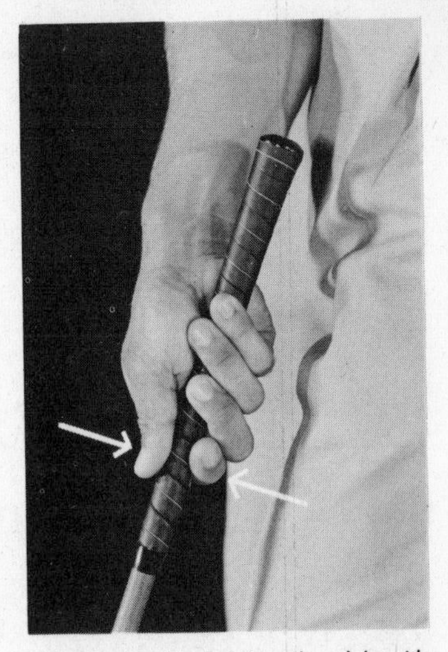

You are actually holding the club with slight pressure between your thumb and forefinger. The other three fingers simply feel the shaft and give you control.

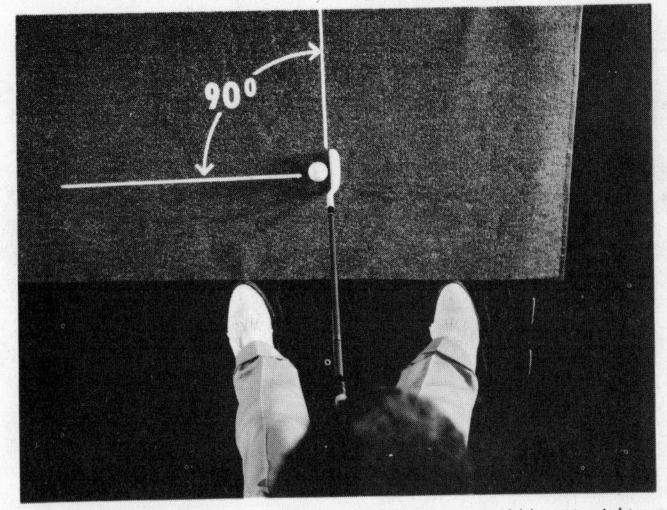

Many good putters feel a better grip by letting the forefinger of the left hand overlap the fingers of the right hand to make the two hands work as one.

The club face should be at a right angle with the intended line of your putt.

There are two methods of putting—wrist putting and firm wrist putting. Beginning golfers usually find the firm wrist putt more effective.

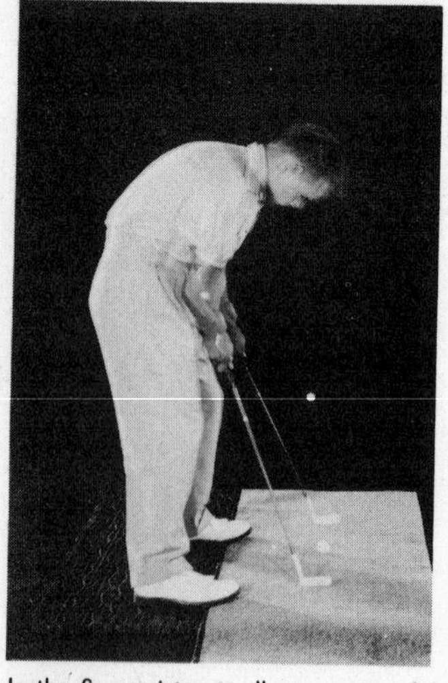

In the firm wrist putt all movement of the putt swing is in your arms . . . no wrist movement . . . just arms swinging from the shoulders with your elbows held in close to your sides. There are two methods of striking the ball and you must select the one best suited to you.

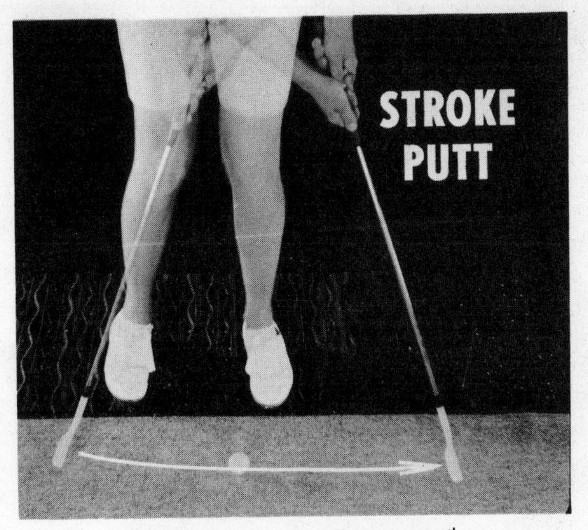

The stroke putt is one continuous, smooth stroke through the ball, the club following through the same distance as the length of the back stroke. It's a longer, smoother stroke.

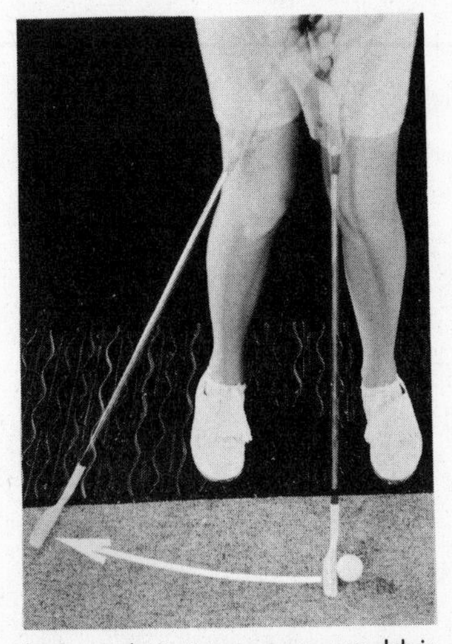

In the stroke putt, you move your club in a low, wide arc, parallel to the ground, in the backswing, along the intended line of flight. Then, reverse the movement . . .

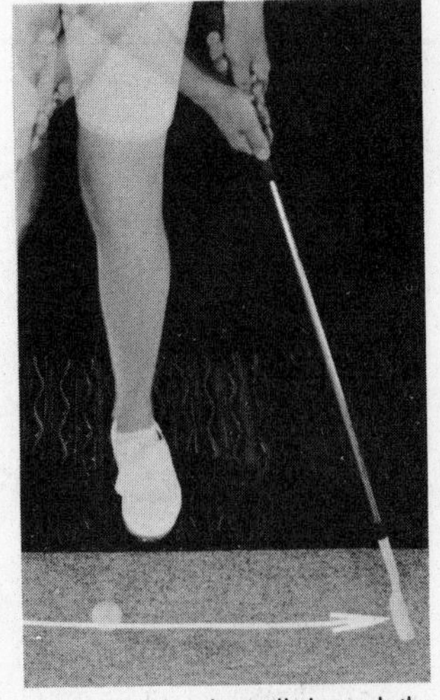

The clubhead stays low all through the forward swing. It's a smooth flowing forward movement through the ball. The clubhead never lifts. And the extended follow-through swings straight through.

The tap putt is a swing that comes up to the ball, taps it with a crisp movement, and then follows after the ball a short way along the direction line . . . not a full follow-through . . . and not one smooth flowing swing. As the name implies, it's a tap . . . but the club does move forward slightly after the tap.

The tap putt is different in that the momentum of the club expends itself in a very short follow-up. You tap the ball forward and your clubhead swings forward naturally, after the tap. There is no conscious follow-through.

You move the club back along the direction line, close to the ground and using only your arms . . . no wrist action.

Then you tap forward toward the ball . . . a thrusting movement . . . low and flat along the direction line. The ball is **tapped** forward.

The thrusting movement of your club accelerates through the ball and expends itself. It follows along the direction line a very short distance. You feel the movement most in your right hand and arm.

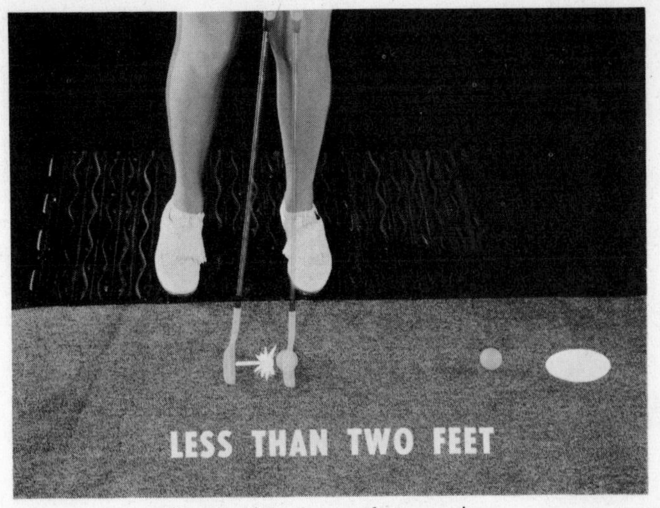

For putts of less than two feet or so, there is no follow-up at all. Just a gentle tap action and your forward movement stops at the ball.

For medium putts, say up to fifteen feet, the short backward movement changes direction into a brisk tap action. You accelerate with a thrusting action through the ball.

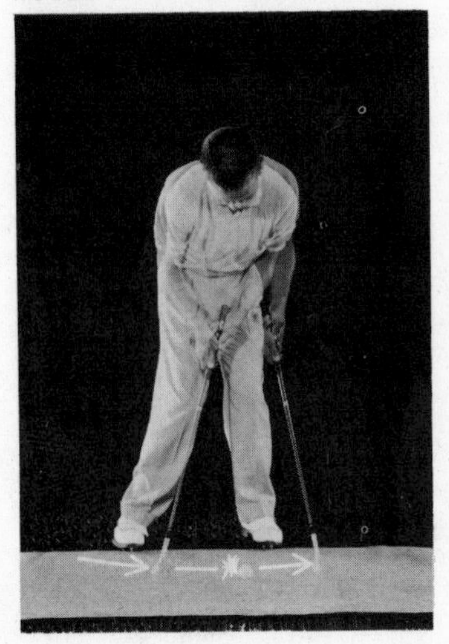

For long putts you'll take a longer backward movement . . . then a longer stroke building up to a smart blow through the ball.

Whatever method you use, tap or stroke, your putting action will follow the same pattern. First, you'll sight your putt, drawing a direction line from the cup back to your ball.

Then, without hesitation, you'll take your address position over the ball. In putting, as in swinging, you must maintain momentum. You've already overcome inertia. Now you must stay in movement.

As you line up your feet and shoulders with the direction line, you keep your clubhead moving up and down behind the ball . . . keeping your momentum. Take your stance . . . sight the direction line . . . and . . .

. . . putt. The time between taking your address position and finishing the putt must not be prolonged . . . not more than two or three seconds. If you take longer than necessary, you'll probably introduce doubt and indecision and you will not perform up to your best.

In all putting you have two concerns combining into a single objective . . . distance and line.

On long putts, your primary objective should be distance . . . moving the ball close enough to the cup that on the next putt your ball is almost certain to go into the cup.

On short putts, your primary concern is line . . . that one sure line to the cup.

But not all greens are level so not all putts are straight. There are many combinations of rolls and slants on greens and you will have to adapt.

For instance, on a slanting green your ball lies directly below the cup. You have an uphill putt.

Here you adapt by adding extra strength to your putt to overcome the force of gravity working against you. It's as though you were putting toward a hole farther away.

But here gravity will be working **with** you . . . a downhill putt where your ball is directly above the cup.

In this case you adapt by lightening your grip . . . softening your stroke . . . as though you were putting to an imaginary hole closer to you.

Now, here's another challenge . . . a sidehill putt where, on a slanting green your ball is off to one side of the direct fall line of the hill.

With a normal straight putt, gravity will start pulling your ball downhill as its speed slows down.

You can compensate by judging the downhill pull and aiming toward a point above the hole. This is called borrowing and is one good way of adjusting to a sidehill lie.

But there's another way that is also very accurate. Let's take the right to left line first.

Now, estimate your direction line . . . a judgment you must make based on your estimate of the downhill pull.

Take your stance so the ball is back a little from your normal ball position . . . back of your left heel.

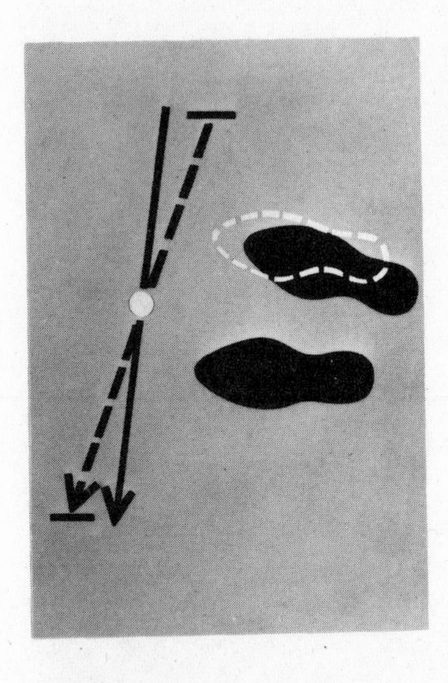

Pull your right foot back slightly.

Then, on your backswing, bring your clubhead back inside the direction line and swing forward across the line, keeping your clubhead square to the direction line.

This produces a sharper break in your ball and, with practice, you'll find you can gauge the strength of your stroke to make the ball break accurately and roll downhill to the cup.

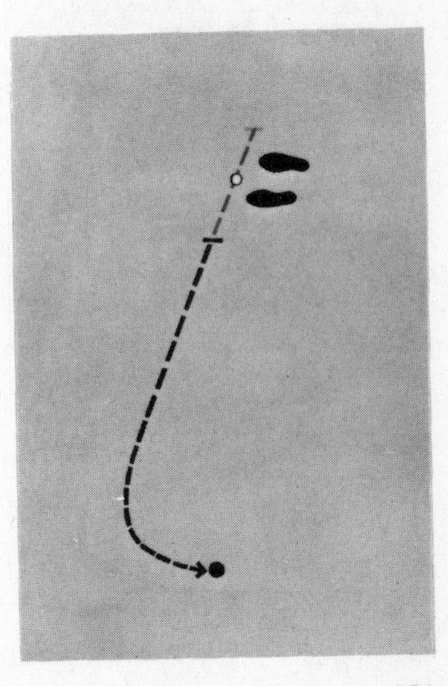

Here's a left to right situation . . . a sidehill lie with the downhill pull to the right. In this case the technique is reversed.

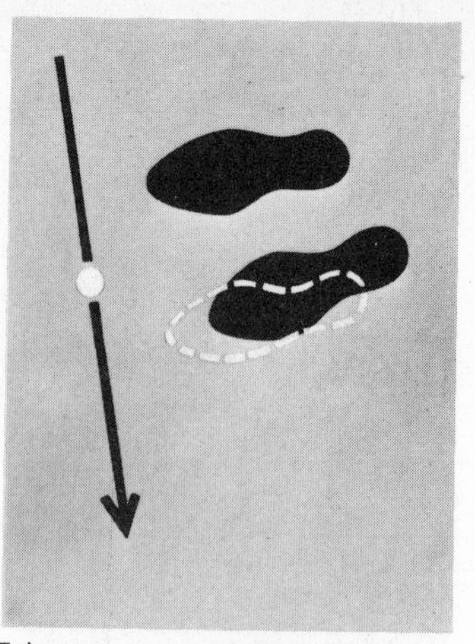

Take your stance with the ball forward a little . . . about opposite your left toe . . . and move your left foot back.

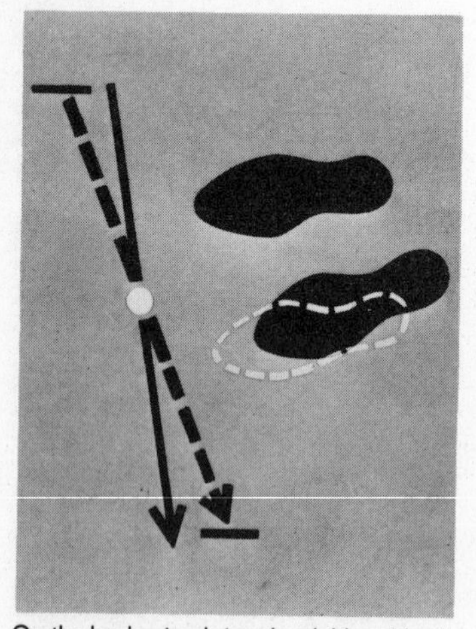

On the backswing bring the clubhead back outside the direction line and swing forward across the line to the inside.

Now the ball travels straight until it loses most of its forward momentum and then breaks toward the hole. This is one of the most challenging putts . . . and one of the most satisfying when you're doing your best.

How good is your best? Only you can know. And you will only know after hours and hours of practice.

6

THE COURTESY AND ETIQUETTE OF GOLF

All over the world, golf grows even greater in popularity. Ability to play the game, heeding its code of sportsmanship, is an asset in health, temperament, and in social and business life. And the finest of golf's benefits is the fun you'll have in the open air, on the rich turf, at the "game of a lifetime."

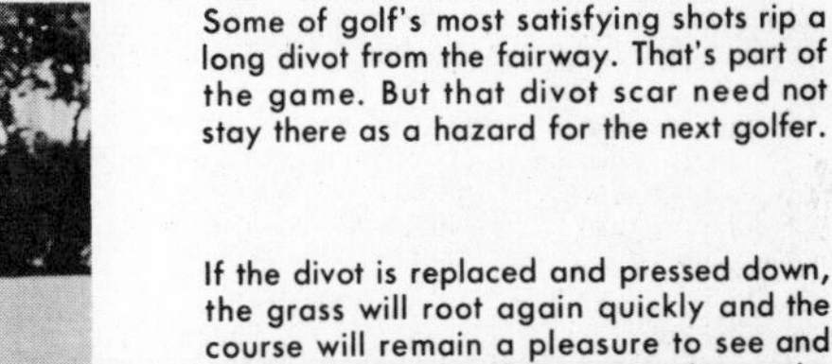

Some of golf's most satisfying shots rip a long divot from the fairway. That's part of the game. But that divot scar need not stay there as a hazard for the next golfer.

If the divot is replaced and pressed down, the grass will root again quickly and the course will remain a pleasure to see and play on. Most golfers try to leave the course better than they found it.

An explosion shot from a trap is a real thrill when your lie gives you a sporting chance to make it.

But a lie in some inconsiderate golfer's footprint requires more than average skill.

It only takes a few seconds to smooth out the marks you make in a trap . . . even if there isn't a rake available, you can back out and smooth your prints with your feet and club.